T0058809

THE IDEAS THAT
MADE AMERICA

The Ideas That Made America

A Brief History

Jennifer Ratner-Rosenhagen

OXFORD
UNIVERSITY PRESS

OXFORD
UNIVERSITY PRESS

Oxford University Press is a department of the University of Oxford. It furthers
the University's objective of excellence in research, scholarship, and education
by publishing worldwide. Oxford is a registered trademark of Oxford University
Press in the UK and certain other countries.

Published in the United States of America by Oxford University Press
198 Madison Avenue, New York, NY 10016, United States of America.

© Oxford University Press 2019

Library of Congress Cataloging-in-Publication Data
Names: Ratner-Rosenhagen, Jennifer, author.
Title: The ideas that made America : a brief history / Jennifer Ratner-Rosenhagen.
Description: New York, NY : Oxford University Press, [2019] |
Includes bibliographical references and index.
Identifiers: LCCN 2018027744 (print) | LCCN 2018048434 (ebook) |
ISBN 9780190625375 (updf) | ISBN 9780190625382 (epub) |
ISBN 9780190625368 (hardback : alk. paper)
Subjects: LCSH: United States—Intellectual life. | United States—History.
Classification: LCC E169.1 (ebook) | LCC E169.1 .R35 2019 (print) |
DDC 973—dc23 LC record available at https://lccn.loc.gov/2018027744

9 8

Printed by Integrated Books International, United States of America

In memory of Merle Curti and Paul Boyer

CONTENTS

CONTENTS

ACKNOWLEDGMENTS

Even brief histories require extensive assistance to bring them into being. Support for this book came in many forms, from feedback at the early stages of its conceptualization to help with research tasks as well as comments and suggestions on various drafts of the manuscript. I am so grateful for the contributions of Laird Boswell, Zoë Rose Buonaiuto, Charlie Capper, Charles Cohen, Vaneesa Cook, George Cotkin, Bill Cronon, Richard Wightman Fox, Sam Gee, David Hollinger, Daniel Hummel, Sari Judge, Michael Kazin, Jim Kloppenberg, Bruce Kuklick, Susan Laufenberg, Isaac Lee, Leonora Neville, Kamila Orlova, Dean Robbins, Daniel Rodgers, Ulrich Rosenhagen, Dorothy Ross, Jennifer Stitt, Madelyn Sundquist, Kevin Walters, Robert Westbrook, and Caroline Winterer. I want to thank the generous and resourceful archivists and librarians who helped me turn research trails from cold to hot and dead ends into breakthroughs: Rebecca Jewett, Tony Lattis, Anita Mechler, Robin Rider, and Lisa Wettelson. I am especially indebted to Nancy Toff, who invited me to take on this project and offered me invaluable advice and encouragement along the way, and to Elizabeth Vaziri and Julia Turner for their roles in shepherding the manuscript through production. The generous support from the University of Wisconsin–Madison's William F. Vilas Trust and the H. I. Romnes

Faculty Fellowship Award provided me the time and resources necessary to complete the book.

To my loving family, Ulrich, Amelie, and Jonah, I say "thank you" again and again for tolerating a home choked with books and notepads, cold sandwiches for dinner, and a matriarch whose imagination too often drifted to remote places and people in American history while she was supposed to be watching them play little league (Jonah), relishing their theater performance (Amelie), or simply listening to them talk about their workday (Ulrich). I am so grateful that my mother, Miriam Ratner, was an English major back in the day when grammar was taught to students and that she was so willing to generously share her expertise as she read through all of her daughter's drafts. I thank my wonderful students at the University of Wisconsin–Madison who taught me whatever I know about communicating my passion for this material. And these acknowledgments would be sorely incomplete were I not to express my deepest gratitude to the extraordinary scholars in American intellectual history, whose imaginative, innovative, and meticulous research has informed my narrative here and whose books are listed in the further reading section. I would feel that this book did its job if it were read as an invitation to further explorations in these and other engaging works of American intellectual history.

This book is dedicated to the extraordinary historians Merle Curti and Paul Boyer, two of my intellectual history predecessors at the University of Wisconsin–Madison. I never met Merle Curti, but I am so fortunate to occupy the chair named for him and thus to have him as a source of daily inspiration in my writing and my teaching. For readers interested in a longer account of American intellectual history, I recommend starting with his majestic, Pulitzer Prize–winning *Growth of American Thought* (1944). I did, however, have the good fortune of meeting Paul Boyer, who welcomed me when I arrived at Madison in 2006 and graced me with his brilliant mind, deep humanity, and beautiful friendship. This book is dedicated to their memory.

THE IDEAS THAT
MADE AMERICA

Introduction

The Ideas That Made America is a brief survey of some of the most compelling episodes and abiding preoccupations in American intellectual history. While I would like to imagine that a book on the history of American thought can be as straightforward as it is accessible, I have been teaching this material long enough to know that this is not always the case. With equal parts intrigue and skepticism, students often ask me: what *is* American intellectual history?

The official version of American intellectual history goes something like this: it is an approach to understanding the American past by way of ideas and the people who made or were moved by them. Intellectual history seeks to understand where certain persistent concerns in American thought have come from and why some ideas, which were important in the past, have faded from view. It can focus on the very particular: a single concept (say, "freedom" or "justice") or a larger body of thought ("democratic theory" or "antislavery"). Histories of thought can also study a particular field of knowledge, such as philosophy, psychology, or sociology, and examine how those disciplines have changed over time. All of these angles into Americans' ways of thinking are used with a careful attention to time and place: Why did they come to those conclusions? Why *then*? Why *there*? For an intellectual historian, the context of the idea is as important as the idea itself. Intellectual history also concerns itself with the myriad institutions that are sites of intellectual production (universities, publishing houses, and think tanks), as well as the various practices people have employed to engage ideas (reading, writing, discussing, experimenting, and so on).

Though ideas, intellectuals, and intellectual movements are the focus in the history of American thought, it is still first and foremost a historical pursuit that adopts all the habits of mind familiar to political, economic, and environmental historians. Intellectual history may even focus on politics, economics, and the environment. But instead of using political parties, an economic depression, or weather patterns to understand American history at a particular time and place, it would approach political history by examining the ideas in a political treatise or presidential address. Its approach to economic history might be to investigate how economists interpreted the cause of a financial downturn or how unemployed laborers made sense of their difficult circumstances. And its approach to the history of the environment might consider the arguments environmental activists used to try to protect endangered species or the way a poet drew symbols from nature in her or his work.

So that is something like the official version of American intellectual history, and, I think, an accurate description of the enterprise. But had it been described to me this way before I knew anything of the subject, I am not quite sure I would have chosen it as my life's work.

The reason I became interested in American intellectual history, why it still holds my attention, why I love teaching it, and why my students seem to share the thrill of it is that it is a way to eavesdrop on the past. Its intent is not to spy on the inner thoughts of unsuspecting dead people. Rather, it is fueled by the desire to come into contact with interesting people we might not otherwise know but for the records of their minds they left behind. This historical sensibility gladly welcomes any source to use for eavesdropping: legal documents, novels, private letters, diaries, photographs, or a painting. No source need be too imposing—like a major tome of theological disputation. And no source is too insignificant—like marginalia in a text or an advertisement in a magazine. Though this book tends to rely on more traditional sources of intellectual history (works of philosophy, political and social theory, literature, and cultural criticism), it hopes to show that these are only some of the sources that can awaken us to all the ways Americans have constructed their realities and made meaning in their lives.

In trying to access the mental and moral worlds of people from the past, *The Ideas That Made America* asks questions about the possibilities for and limits on doing so. It raises questions such as the following: Is it possible to fully understand the intellectual motivations of historical actors? Can we apprehend how or why ideas have had the power to make Americans change their minds about—or take action on—a particular issue? How can we measure the influence of historical actors' ideas on social, political, and economic conditions (and vice versa)? By posing such questions, this book invites thinking about thinking. But more important, it seeks to demonstrate that thinking is where so much of the historical action is.

This story opens with the first contacts between European explorers and Native Americans in the late fifteenth century and carries the narrative up to American intellectual life today. Professional thinkers, sophisticated arguments, and intellectual classics are present here, but so are lay Christians, simplistic arguments, and ephemera. They are all here because they reflect the richly varied sources and expressions of Americans' intellects. These chapters attempt to portray some of the excitement of accessing American history through ideas and to interpret how Americans throughout history have understood themselves, their nation, and their world.

This book tells the story of developments in American intellectual life as a history of "crossings" in all of their varieties—between one cultural setting and another, text and context, secular analysis and sacred belief, and formal argument and emotional affirmation. Of all the types of intellectual transfer this book will focus on, three stand out as the most important.

The movement of ideas across national borders. American intellectual history is filled with expatriates, émigrés, and foreign texts, and so of prime importance here is how Americans' intellectual and moral worlds have long been the products of transnational crossings. Therefore, some of this history takes place "off stage": in early modern Europe at the time of Europeans' first contacts with the indigenous peoples of the New World or on the Galápagos Islands in the nineteenth century when a young Charles Darwin first noticed something strange about the finches on the archipelago. Also crucial are intellectuals who moved off and on the American stage. Just one example is D. T. (Daisetsu Teitaro) Suzuki, who lived and worked with the philosopher Paul Carus in Illinois in the early twentieth century, learning everything he could about American religion and culture, before returning to the United States at mid century as the ambassador of Zen Buddhism to the West.

The movement of ideas across temporal borders. Ideas are products of their time and place, but they also go on to influence future intellectual movements. For example, late twentieth-century postcolonialist thought drew on turn-of-the-last-century Pan-African discourses, while second-wave feminists took their inspiration from their nineteenth-century American foremothers, who themselves got their inspiration from classical antiquity. In addition, major texts have afterlives. John Eliot, for example, remade the Bible—a text composed well over a millennium earlier—for seventeenth-century Algonquian Indians, and Elizabeth Cady Stanton took the Declaration of Independence of 1776 and turned it into the Declaration of Sentiments in 1848. Kahlil Gibran's *The Prophet* reveals both the concerns of an American immigrant in 1923 and those of American soldiers fighting abroad during World War II (who read the Armed Services Edition of his book).

The movement of ideas across borders within American culture. Ideas, patterns of thought, and rigorous modes of inquiry are not the provenance of "highbrow" thinkers only. They can be found in "popular" culture as well. True, some professional intellectuals worried about tiny logical distinctions and articulated the results of their inquiry in a highly technical language. But they also had their critics who complained that intellectual engagement demanded a widening of intellectual horizons and a more compelling way of communicating their findings to a broader public. A full appreciation of American intellectual life requires attention to debates among elites, as well as concerns expressed in what the great twentieth-century writer Ralph Ellison called our culture's "lower frequencies."[1]

This may seem like an awful lot of moving around, but that is what is required to capture a faithful picture of the ideas that made America. Intellectual history is invariably a history of other times and other places, because historical actors do not just think in their moment and in their tiny spot on planet Earth. They also live in an ideational realm where they are communing with thinkers or moral worlds from elsewhere. Take Martin Luther King Jr., for example. It is important to know that he was inspired by Mahatma Gandhi, and that Gandhi was a fervent reader of Henry David Thoreau, and that Thoreau took a deep interest in fourteenth-century Buddhist texts. So to understand King's theology, do we need to familiarize ourselves with ancient Buddhism? Not necessarily, although it would not hurt. The point here is simply that in order to capture the imaginations of thinkers from the past, we need to be as intellectually peripatetic as they were.

Ideas are never frozen in their time and place, nor are they vapors that float in some otherworldly, transcendent realm. Rather, they are historical forces that move—and thereby change—from one interlocutor to another, one place to another, and even one time period to another. To be sure, throughout our history, many Americans have exalted ideas like democracy, freedom, and equality, while others experienced them as fighting words meant to deny them their benefits. But these ideas have achieved their power not because their meanings are absolute but precisely because they are so fluid, so multivalent, and so prone to redefinition when they come into new conditions of possibility. The vibrancy of American thought lies in the movement of ideas as they have been enlisted to mean different things to different people throughout the American past.

With all of this talk of the past, it may seem that the present is far from view. Intellectual history does deal very much with America today. But it understands that our current political debates, economic fetishes, and moral commitments all have histories. And so, as a result, today's America is the result neither of nature nor of necessity; it is the creation of historical circumstance, chance, accident, human folly, and wisdom, and sometimes all of these together. What most concerns us today might have seemed ludicrous to our ancestors. And what our ancestors perceived as having great urgency might have somehow become irrelevant for us. Why? That is what intellectual history tries to figure out. In seeking the answers, we achieve a little epistemic humility, which is indeed humbling, but also strangely energizing and ennobling.

Chapter 1

World of Empires: Precontact–1740

In the beginning was the word and the word was "America." The year was 1507, and the place, Saint-Dié-des-Vosges, in the northwest of today's France. It first appeared in a book titled, in short form, *Cosmographiae Introductio* (the original title was forty-eight words long). The anonymous author set out to cover the known world, including new lands unknown to Ptolemy but later discovered by Amerigo Vespucci. Much of the book covered information familiar to early sixteenth-century readers, such as the knowledge that the moon, the sun, and the planets all revolved around the earth. The author also fit new information into familiar frames, explaining how discussion of Asia, Africa, and Europe must be updated now that they have "been more extensively explored." But then he[1] mentioned a little-known "fourth part [that] has been discovered by Amerigo Vespucci." He suggested, "inasmuch as both Europe and Asia received their names from women, I see no reason why anyone should justly object to calling this part Amerige, i.e., the land of Amerigo, or America, after Amerigo, its discoverer, a man of great ability."[2] Accompanying the book was a massive folded map— when opened, it measured four and a half by eight feet—showing familiar continents and, for the very first time, a new one: a narrow landmass, impressively long (roughly as long as Africa from north to south) with its manly appellation "America" on the southern half.

Seventeenth- and eighteenth-century British colonial thinkers do not appear to have been familiar with this obscure map, though they knew of Vespucci. But Vespucci's significance faded for them as they

Martin Waldseemüller's 1507 map of the world was the first to use the name "America" (found on the westernmost portion of the map). *Detail, Universalis Cosmographia Secundum Ptholomaei Traditionem et Americi Vespucii Alioru[m]que Lustrationes, [St. Dié], Geography and Map Division, Library of Congress*

sought to make sense of their history. When they viewed American history, they did so through the lens of empire in general, not by focusing on the explorers that empires sent out into the world. The medieval notion of *translatio imperii* (translation of empire)—a vision of a grand historical imperial line of succession from Alexander the Great to Rome, from the Romans to Charlemagne's Franks, and so on—framed their views of America in the larger course of world history. From their vantage point, it seemed that America was what this line of succession was leading up to.

Early European Americans' assessment of themselves as the beneficiaries of this grand historical imperial lineage required that they adopt a rather partisan perspective on history. This view omits the fact that for much of early America, Spain and France also had imperial claims on the continent—and in some areas an even stronger footing than Britain. In the sixteenth and early seventeenth century, all of the European powers' colonial ventures in North America had slow and fitful beginnings. None of them came with any intention of establishing permanent colonies. After all, colonization was an expensive and risky venture. They simply wanted settlements to anchor their expeditions and to direct the flow of goods, and for the godly among them to find some souls for Christ along the way.

However, the allure of the idea of *translatio imperii* clearly overpowered the harsh reality of establishing the English (after 1707, British) Empire on the ground. The British were the last to this process of exploration and had some of its most difficult trials and spectacular failures, and though they were the first to establish a colony in Jamestown in 1607, that experiment did not get off to an auspicious start (with 440 of the estimated 500 colonists dying from disease and starvation). It was not until well after the French hunkered down in Quebec in 1608 and the Spanish in Santa Fe in 1610 that persecuted Puritans and Quakers in England looked to the New World as a place in which they might be able to live and worship as they pleased. They risked the hazards of transatlantic travel and confronted an uncertain future in a strange land not to spearhead the mission of British imperialism, but to escape religious persecution.

For the notion of *translatio imperii* to have any purchase, it had to work its way around not only the formidable Spanish and French imperial claims throughout large portions of North America but also—and more conspicuously—the fact that all the explorers on behalf of European empires arrived on a continent of sprawling indigenous empires, such as the Powhatan Confederacy in Virginia, the Iroquois Confederacy east of the Mississippi, and the Algonquian tribes' alliances all around the Great Lakes. The leaders of these native empires likely knew nothing of the concept of *translatio imperii*, but they certainly had a stake in proving it wrong.

Thus, the presence of tens of millions of indigenous people whose ancestors had lived on the continent for ten thousand years suggests that the story of American intellectual history might require a very different beginning...

In the beginning there were words, likely thousands of them, perhaps tens of thousands, or even more. They were the words spoken by the estimated one thousand to two thousand distinct linguistic communities among the roughly fifty million (some scholars suggest a hundred million) indigenous people living in the Americas at the dawn of European colonization. The vast majority of these words are lost to history. What we do know with a high degree of certainty is that the word *America* prior to the arrival of European explorers and settlers was not one of them.

Historians lack knowledge not only of the words spoken by millions of indigenous Americans at the time of European contact but also of the ideas and worldviews they once expressed. There is a paucity of surviving historical sources, and those that do exist are either mute, inaudible, or unreliable as they were penned by missionaries and explorers, not the natives themselves. This is not to say that we know nothing of their ways of life and practices. Quite the opposite is true. For over a hundred years, archeologists and ethnologists have pieced together rich and in some cases very detailed information drawn from surviving pictographs, decorative beads, weapons carved from stone, ritual objects, and burial mounds. More recently, paleoethnobotanists (botanists who focus on findings at archeological sites) have studied petrified seeds and plant remains to develop a fuller picture of different native communities' agriculture and diet, while epidemiologists have studied bones and teeth to learn what they can about diseases and mortality rates. In addition, a variety of scholars have used written records and oral traditions from later periods to fill in details from earlier periods. But none of this reveals much at all about how native people made sense of the arrival of Europeans, not to mention how they made sense of themselves and their worlds prior to contact.

If the conditions were more favorable for starting a brief history of American intellectual life from the vantage point of Native Americans, the tale of the ideas that made America would ideally commence with this alternative beginning, and it would start even earlier than with the arrival of Europeans. In this version, Native Americans would figure as historical subjects and not objects of Europeans' analysis and scrutiny. But as intellectual history seeks to recover and interpret ideas, and preferably from reliable evidence whenever possible, this study will privilege the beginning for which there is much sturdier and more extensive documentation.

There is, nevertheless, a crucial insight to be drawn from this situation. It is that, throughout history, people's ideas and ways of understanding sometimes lose their power or die out altogether, not because better ideas and ways of understanding proved them inadequate, but because they are silenced by means other than rational argument and reasoned debate. We may speak of a "war of ideas," which may have truth to it, but only as metaphor. In the case of Native American ideas during the first century of contact with Europeans, it was actual physical warfare—violent, bloody warfare—as well as disease and loss of land, that drove their ways of understanding to fade from historical memory.

As different as these two beginnings of this history are, both demonstrate that any intellectual history of America must begin in this world of early modern empires. In doing so, they demonstrate that American intellectual life got its start as much within the minds of Europeans as in the external arena of fractious competing empires, each with its own history and uncertainty about its future along these jagged and shifting contact zones.

And yet to talk of something like an "American intellectual life" in this era is to talk rubbish. In the minds of the earliest settlers and colonizers they did not belong to "America" but rather to their home countries and to their local companions in their tiny enclaves, which they knew were surrounded—and dramatically outnumbered—by indigenous people whom they referred to as "Indians." Just as they had no deep connection to something called "America," they also had no shared set of ideas or beliefs, no shared loyalties, because they had no common nationality, religion, or historical memory. To the best of historians' knowledge, their only common intellectual project was to draw new boundaries around their moral communities, and to cling to old identities and negotiate new ones in the face of such motley neighbors and an unpredictable future.

Intellectual Consequences of the Americas for Europe

In the centuries after Waldseemüller's map, letters, personal testimony, travel accounts, and cartographic information would help fill out the contours of Europeans' image of America. But the dizzying plethora of information raised far more questions than it answered, and pressed European observers to rethink their intellectual conventions regarding the natural world, history, and God and his creation. The communications, reports, and promotional efforts of Sir Walter Raleigh, Thomas Harriot, and Richard Hakluyt the younger would help reveal a world both wondrous and terrifying. In time, their accounts would be followed by many more fantastical versions of strange people and exotic terrain, supplemented with curious specimens and illustrations, awakening an unquenchable curiosity among educated European laypeople and governmental administrators too powerful for church authorities to contain.

Europeans interpreted information from America to fit existing schema. But even those efforts at correspondence strained the familiar contours of political, social, religious, and scientific thought. While it was commonplace for European observers to see a continent full of heathens as an opportunity to further Christ's mission, many felt pressed to reassess various aspects of Scripture and their classical heritage in light of those heathens.

One big problem concerned how to reckon time and space. For theologian Isaac LaPeyrère, a French Marrano, information about native populations in the New World sufficiently challenged the accuracy of Genesis. This information helped him to conclude in his *Prae-Adamitae* (1655) that the presence of human life halfway across the globe must have meant that men existed before Adam. For the Dominican philosopher Tommaso Campanella, Columbus's reports made clear that hell must not be on the other side of the globe, so he deferred to Augustine's view that it must lie at the center of the earth. Joseph Justus Scaliger, the famous late sixteenth-century Italian scholar who had devised the Julian period, which reconciled the discrepancies among the solar, lunar, and Indiction cycles and reset Christ's birth at 4713 BC, incorporated knowledge about indigenous American temporalities gleaned from explorers in his 1583 *Opus de emendatione temporum*. And Jesuit explorer José de Acosta had to "laugh" at the inaccuracy of Aristotle's *Meteorology*, which was then still taught in European colleges. When he and his crew crossed the equator en route to the "Indies" (South America), instead of experiencing "violent heat" per Aristotle's theories, they were chilled to the bone.[3]

Another problem was how knowledge about Native Americans would affect the Europeans' conceptions of human nature. The most common strategy for them was to use Native Americans as evidence of the superiority of their God, culture, language, and physical attributes. But that strategy did not work for everyone, as a few holdouts, acknowledging the diversity of native peoples and cultures, demanded that settled truths become unsettled, and that skepticism and even a little relativism were the only appropriate responses.

No early modern philosopher was more intent on using reports about natives to critically appraise his own society than the French philosopher and essayist Michel de Montaigne. Having never traveled to the New World, he learned about it by talking with some natives taken to France by a royal expedition, as well as his manservant, who had spent ten years in Brazil. With the help of these informants, Montaigne formulated some of the earliest ideas of the "noble savage." His "Apology for Raymond Sebond" highlighted the diversity of moral perspectives and cultural practices of indigenous Americans, paving the way for "On Cannibals" (1580), an essay that excoriated Europeans for their ethnocentrism. For Montaigne, the New World's rumored cannibalism seemed more understandable than the daily barbarisms of the Old, where corrupt Europeans, driven by material acquisitions, waged war to steal lands they neither needed nor deserved. He thus employed indigenous peoples to challenge the limits and chauvinism of European culture while stressing the need to understand other people's beauty and dignity.

Across the English Channel, Thomas Hobbes had a much less favorable view of the natives, but he used them similarly to appraise the problems of early modern European notions of government. In his classic, *Leviathan* (1651), Hobbes employed the symbol of the Indian to establish the dangers of a society founded on the "ill condition [of] meer Nature." In such circumstances, he warned, "there is no place for Industry; because the fruit thereof is uncertain: and consequently no Culture of the Earth; no Navigation . . . no Knowledge of the face of the Earth; no account of Time; no Arts; no Letters . . . the life of man [is] solitary, poore, nasty, brutish, and short." For European readers who were skeptical that such a society ever existed, Hobbes recommended that they consider the American Indian: "For the savage people in many places of *America*, . . . have no government at all." He emphasized that this disturbing picture of society is not a thing of the past because American savages "live at this day in that brutish manner."[4]

The traffic of information about the fauna of the New World similarly encouraged European natural philosophers in the sixteenth and seventeenth centuries to revise significant portions of their biological classifications, some inherited from antiquity. Eyewitness accounts and drawings of vegetation, even by those with no credentials as natural philosophers, forced established authorities to cede some credit for scientific advancement to New World intellectual novices. But early modern European philosophers and theologians had more to worry about than their own intellectual authority. They had to overcome feeling besieged by the torrent of new information and figure out how to keep pace. (One measure of the new findings' scope is that the number of known plants multiplied fortyfold from the beginning of the seventeenth century to the middle of the eighteenth.) In the case of the New World's botanical bounty, they felt the urge to account for these new findings not just because the plants were beautiful, tasty, or promised therapeutic benefits, but because they held clues to the entire schema of knowledge about the natural world and man's place in it.

Wealthy Europeans devised a way to handle the bumper crop of treasures by curating in their homes curiosity cabinets packed with exotic seedlings and petrified flowers (as well as speckled shells, framed insects, and unidentified teeth). But Europeans' vogue for exhibiting American oddities did not constitute a long-term strategy for mastering the new details of their known world or reassure them that the existence of the strange new world from which these curiosities came had no implications for their understanding of themselves in the cosmic scheme.

Native and European Intellectual Exchanges

Throughout the seventeenth and into the eighteenth century, "America" represented more of an intellectual problem to be solved than a term that evoked stability, affinity, or affection. While colonists

Visual renderings had the power to shape Europeans' imaginations about the New World's inhabitants, but they were susceptible to mistranslation and adaptation. The English artist John White had sustained contact with the Secotan Indians during his two-year stay in what would become North Carolina and tried to document them faithfully in "A Festive Dance" (ca. 1585, left). However, when his representation of a peaceful Indian feast arrived in England, it was reimagined by the English engraver Robert Vaughan as a warlike procession around the captured John Smith in his illustration "Their Triumph about Him" for Smith's *The Generall Historie of Virginia, New-England, and the Summer Isles* (1627, right). *Library of Congress, F229.S59 1907; British Museum, 1906, 0509.1.10*

made proprietary claims on the land, many of them—even those whose families had been in America for generations—expressed abiding feelings of being existentially unmoored in a foreign land. While direct and sustained contact with Native Americans had the power to unsettle European settlers, it also promised them the knowledge necessary for making their way in their new worlds.

Europeans' interest in native languages and cultural practices was often instrumental and self-serving, but colonists recognized them as crucial portals to knowledge about their adopted home-land. As precious for the colonists as squash seeds, beaver pelts, or nuggets of gold were, it was the information about where to find them, how to extract them, and the uses to which they could be put that was most valuable to them. The missionaries and clergy among them understood that these prosaic matters were also windows onto the natives' moral worlds. Knowing their beliefs could help them to find the right fulcrum for converting them to Christianity. And getting them to convert to Christianity would not only save their souls but also help turn potential enemies into allies.

Unlike Spanish Franciscan and French Jesuit missionaries, who went to Indian country in search of souls to convert, Puritans tried to bring the natives to them. The differences lay, in part, in their different conceptions of belonging to the faith. For Catholics, participating in the sacraments, daily prayer, and deferring to the authority and guidance of the clergy were of prime importance, but the ability to read the Bible was not. For non-Anglican Protestants, the ability to read the Bible and receive the Word directly was the alpha and omega of belonging, and so teaching natives how to read was their means for conversion.

The most prominent example of this strategy can be found in Puritan minister John Eliot's effort to establish the first "praying town" where local Algonquian Indians were expected to check their own customs at the gate of entry and, once inside, model their lives on their Christian neighbors'. Eliot held the view, not uncommon for the time, that Native Americans were part of the ten lost tribes of Israel who made their way to the New World. (He later changed his mind about this as he learned more of the Natick language and culture.) Eliot believed that the only way to bring them back to God was to train them to read the Bible for themselves. He thus alphabetized the Algonquian language in order to translate the Bible and eventually other religious texts into prospective converts' native tongue. Many of his fellow Puritan divines greeted this with skepticism as they believed the Word of God—though universal—could not be rendered in so primitive a language. With the help of two

Native American teachers and a printer, he undertook the task of translating the Bible into Massachusett, which they completed in 1663. This was the first bible printed in America.

Because the Bible signified a Logos unto itself, a specific mindset was needed to get one's words right. To train the natives to have well-ordered minds, Eliot followed up his translation with *The Logick Primer* (1672), the first work of philosophy composed in the New World. Written in English and interlined with Massachusett to teach the Algonquian Indians how to align their thinking with Northern European notions and styles of reason, it promised "Logick" (or "Anomayag" as it was referred to in Massachusett), "the Rule, where by every thing, every Speech is composed, analysed, or opened to be known." Eliot's focus on translating the Bible in order to bring indigenous ways of reasoning closer to his reflects the Puritans' persistent concern about disorderly speech. Because for the Puritans the Word was their only portal to spiritual knowledge, written and spoken language had to follow strict rules or else risk wreaking havoc on the community. They were less concerned about sticks and stones breaking bones and worried instead with how words could hurt them. A common Puritan saying was "the Tongue breaketh the Bone."

Eliot was not interested only in passing along the Puritans' beliefs; he was interested in—and sought to put on the historical record—the natives' views as well. However, he took up this task only after they had converted. In *The Dying Speeches of Several Indians* (1685), Eliot recorded a dying man by the name of Piambohou as uttering: "*I* beleive Gods promise, that he will forever save all that belive in Jesus Christ. Oh Lord Jesus helpe me, deliver me and save my soul from Hell, by thine own bloud, which thou hast shed for me." He also recorded the words of a young man named Nehemiah, who lay dying after being attacked by his hunting partner: "Now I desire patiently to take up my crosse and misery. . . . Oh Christ Jesus help me, thou are my Redeemer, my Saviour, and my deliverer: I confesse my selfe a sinner."[5] If these

MAMUSSE
WUNNEETUPANATAMWE
UP-BIBLUM GOD
NANEESWE
NUKKONE TESTAMENT
KAH WONK
WUSKU TESTAMENT.

Ne quoſhkinnumuk naſhpe Wuttinneumoh *CHRIST*
noh aſoowesit

JOHN ELIOT·

CAMBRIDGE:

Printeuoop naſhpe *Samuel Green* kah *Marmaduke Johnson.*

1 6 6 3.

Eliot's Logic Primer

Darkneſs   *upon*   *deep*
3. Pohkenum   woskeche   moonói.

This Affirmative   *general*   *Propo-*
Ne noowae wameyeue pakodtittu-
ſition.
mooonk.

    Spirit   *moved*   *upon*
4. Naſhauanit popomſhau woskeche

waters.   *This Affirmative*   *general*
nippekontu.   Ne   noowae   wameyeue

Propoſition.
pakodtittumooonk.

   All   *ſingle*   *Notions are*
Wame ꞌ ſiyeumꝏe wahittumꝏaſh

    Pairs   *which*   *inlighten*
nequtayittumooaſh niſh wequohtoad-

each other,   *them onely.*
tumooaſh, & niſh webe.

— 26 —

To train New World natives to believe and think like Old World Puritans, missionary John Eliot translated the Bible into Massachusett in 1663 (left) and then wrote *The Logick Primer* (1672, above; figure from 1904 reprint) in Massachusett interlined with English. Though Eliot sought to win souls for Christ, not subjects for Mother England, his translations demonstrate how language was a crucial instrument of European imperialism. *AC6 Eℓ452 663m, Houghton Library, Harvard University; Bible Collection, Rare Book and Special Collections Division, Library of Congress, 6796462* reflect New England Indians' *Weltanschauungen,* then it was only after they had been refashioned to pipe through the Puritans' thought worlds.

Eventually others would try to duplicate Eliot's efforts at mutual understanding and conversion, but the extraordinary linguistic diversity on the continent presented an enormous barrier to doing so. Given the existence of an estimated one thousand to two thousand different indigenous languages, it is no wonder that European observers felt that they were confronted by a most imposing, unscalable Tower of Babel. This was a constant source of exasperation, even for French Jesuits, who (like their brethren around the world) made much greater efforts than their Protestant counterparts to learn the natives' tongues. Frustrated by his failed attempt to communicate with a group of Indians in Illinois country, one Jesuit missionary complained to his superiors, "I spoke to them in six different Languages, of which they understood none."[6] British Protestant settlers did not make a similar effort to learn native languages, and this surely contributed to their chronic fear of being surrounded by chaos. The scale and nature of the linguistic barriers were contributing factors to European encounters with natives ending in violent warfare rather than temperate debate.

However, the difficulties arising from the cacophony of indigenous tongues went far deeper than impeding conversation. Rather, they posed deep and troubling intellectual problems about human nature and natural law for European thinkers. For millennia, the biblical explanation provided in Genesis 11:1 had sufficiently dispelled the mystery about different languages of the globe. The descendants of Noah spoke a common language until they excited the wrath of God with their hubris, and he punished them by depriving them of their shared tongue and leaving them to scatter the earth in their mutually incomprehensible languages. But the enormous scale of linguistic diversity in the New World strained the credulity of the Genesis account, encouraging thinkers to chart new theories about the origins and implications of differences in human languages.

In his "Dissertation on the Origin of the Native Races of America" (1642, Eng. trans. 1884), Hugo Grotius, the Dutch philosopher and inventor of natural law theory, speculated that "men of different races were mingled together," but without a "common government," they broke into linguistic "families [which] framed a vocabulary specially for themselves."[7] Such a view reflected Grotius's search for natural laws that accounted for diversity while revealing a unifying, underlying set of causes. Puritan dissenter Roger Williams had the advantage of living among the Narragansett Indians when he drafted *A Key to the Language of America* (1643). Having been banished from the Massachusetts Bay colony eight years earlier, and having made a home among the natives of Narragansett Bay, Williams was not interested in developing a universal scheme for language or for generalizing about the human condition. Rather, he was interested in what the natives' language could reveal to him about these particular people, at that particular time, in that particular place. Williams's compendia provided an early ethnography of the Narragansetts' daily life, customs, social organization, ethics, and what he described as their natural grace. Given that he was treated with more warmth and compassion among the natives than among his fellow Puritans, the question of which culture was more "civilized" coursed through the book.

From their earliest contacts in the seventeenth century and well into the sustained—if strained—relations in the eighteenth century, European settlers and Native Americans had to find ways to draw information from one another and about one another to ensure their own survival. But one of the most dramatic intellectual consequences of these exchanges was that European settlers came to understand themselves in their new surroundings as a people distinct from the natives. For them, insofar as they saw themselves as "Americans," it was an identity more oppositional than substantial. Their slow and fitful process of becoming Americans meant knowing who they were not long before formulating any clear idea of who they were.

Puritan Intellectual Order in a Disordered American World

The sheer diversity of cultures and local conditions among seventeenth- and early eighteenth-century colonists prevented them from inhabiting a shared intellectual framework. For one thing, they did not come as part of a unified religious group, but as Puritans, Quakers, Huguenots, Catholics, Anglicans, Dutch Reformed, and a variety of other religious dissenters. African slaves brought with them the faith traditions particular to their region of origin: some were polytheists, others believed in a supreme force, while others were animists and pagans, in addition to those who came as Muslim and Christian converts. The extraordinary number and variety of native tribes on the East Coast meant that Protestants and Catholics had more beliefs in common than did the different tribes with each other. For the European transplants, their country of origin was as important as their religious tradition; they identified either as English, Scottish, Dutch, German, or French, when they were not attached to even smaller regional distinctions back home. Add to that the different climates and conditions among the colonies up and down the eastern coastline, each requiring a localized knowledge particular to the area. The demographics varied dramatically too, as seventeenth-century New England towns were populated by families, whereas Virginia and the Lower South were dominated by single men. Schooling and literacy were all over the spectrum, with most Native Americans, indentured servants, African slaves, and even some of their white overseers unable or scarcely able to read and write, while Puritans were some of the most literate—and textually prolific—people on planet Earth.

If they shared one thing, however, it was a profound and steadfast longing to redraw the boundaries of their moral communities in the New World of empires. For European colonists, living in remote outposts of their mother cultures meant that they adopted multifocal habits of attention. They looked eastward across the Atlantic for intellectual products and cultural wares, focused on the demands and expectations of their local communities in the colonies, and scouted the ways of indigenous populations or slaves (or both) to mark differences between themselves and others, all the while reconfiguring their mental and moral coordinates to understand themselves and love their God in light of these claims on their imaginations. For the Native Americans living in close proximity to European colonials, that meant dealing with the psychic rupture brought on by the presence of hostile invaders, their strange customs and tongues and continuous warfare, and the invisible forces unleashing illness, pestilence, and death on their communities. And for African slaves, that meant toggling between metaphysical questions about why the cosmos had delivered them to such a fate and daily pragmatic ones about the hidden rules for survival.

Every one of these communities left some records of these mental and moral struggles. However, none churned out the variety and volume of challenging texts (histories, poems, and jeremiads), founded institutions (such as Harvard College, the colonies' first institution of higher learning, established in 1636), and produced what today would be called "intellectuals" to the degree that Puritan New England did. The list of thinkers with their daunting records of mind is humbling, and includes John Cotton, Increase Mather, Cotton Mather, Jonathan Edwards, and Anne Hutchinson. Their textual and recorded oral claims were invariably theological because their faith structured everything they thought. This was true even in the case of Hutchinson, who insisted that her "own judgement" and "conscience" were forged "by an immediate revelation. . . . By the voice of his own spirit to my soul."[8]

The Puritans were not "puritanical" as this adjective has come to be deployed to refer to prudish, austere, finger-wagging sourpusses. In fact, this meaning of "puritanical" is an early twentieth-century invention dreamed up by literary intellectuals in search of a language to criticize the lingering Victorianism they saw as a threat to their intellectual experimentation. But given documents like Edwards's "Sinners in the Hands of an Angry God" sermon of 1741, it is easy to see how they might have gotten that impression:

> The God that holds you over the pit of Hell, much as one holds
> a spider, or some loathsome insect, over the fire, abhors you, and
> is dreadfully provoked; his wrath towards you burns like fire; he
> looks upon you as worthy of nothing else, but to be cast into the
> fire; he is of purer eyes than to bear to have you in his sight; you are
> ten thousand times so abominable in his eyes as the most hateful
> venomous serpent is in ours.[9]

And yet considering the ravishing power of Edwards's language and imagery, it is hard to see how those young intellectuals could not recognize that in him they had a dazzling literary exemplar.

The Puritans also were the first colonists to develop philosophy as a formal practice of systematic thought in early America. Although suffused in supernatural understandings of the world, the Puritans did not believe that there was an insoluble tension between their religious worldview and scientific investigation. Indeed, it is because the Puritan religious imagination envisioned humanity as completely enveloped by the towering presence of an omniscient, all-powerful deity that their theology could stress the duty to acquire knowledge. Logic, mathematics, and natural philosophy all helped access the manifestations of God's will in the world around them. They believed that salvation required a heart informed by a well-ordered mind, which was the precondition for receiving biblical truths. The commitment to a "covenant" theology, which reconciled divine rule and human reason, was evident in the intellectual preoccupations of Increase Mather and his son, Cotton. In *Catechismus Logicus* (1675), the elder Mather reveals the role of logic and rhetoric in ministerial training at Harvard College; his son's *The Christian Philosopher* (1721) a half

century later shows the persistent effort of Puritan divines to en-
list logic and science in the worship of the supernatural order of
the world.

Jonathan Edwards brought philosophy to a whole new level,
incorporating ontology, epistemology, and ethics to create the
most comprehensive and formidable intellectual system of
prerevolutionary America. As his "Sinners in the Hands of an Angry
God" sermon shows, his reputation as a fire-and-brimstone New
Lights leader of the First Great Awakening who took delight in
terrorizing unregenerate Calvinists may be warranted. But he was
also an exacting Platonist who exerted a deep and lasting influence
on American speculative thought. Edwards was greatly influenced
by Isaac Newton and John Locke. He drew from Newton's *Principia*
(1687) an empirical natural theology he could bring to bear on
Calvinist theology; from *Opticks* (1704) a conception of God as
radiating light, the Invisible making things visible; and from John
Locke's notion of sense experience in *An Essay Concerning Human
Understanding* (1690) a new mode of spiritual cognizance, which
Edwards referred to as a "sense of the heart." Ever struggling between heart and head, Edwards envisioned a balance of power in
sanctified reason.

Of all the Puritan texts whose luminous phrasing is well
remembered but subtle argument long forgotten, John Winthrop's
"Modell of Christian Charity" sermon has no rival. As Winthrop
told his fellow Puritan refugees in 1630:

> For wee must Consider that wee shall be as a Citty upon a Hill, the
> eies of all people are uppon us; soe that if wee shall deale falsely
> with our god in this worke wee have undertaken and soe cause
> him to withdrawe his present help from us, wee shall be made a
> story and a byword through the world, wee shall open the mouthes
> of enemies to speake evill of the wayes of god and all professours
> for Gods sake; wee shall shame the faces of many of gods worthy
> servants, and cause theire prayers to be turned into Cursses upon

us till wee be consumed out of the good land whether wee are goeing.[10]

It is not wrong to read this as a statement of the Puritans' sense of moral mission and exceptionalism as they embarked on new lives in a new land. It is, however, problematic to read it as a statement about *America's* moral mission and exceptionalism (which has become the conventional interpretation since Ronald Reagan popularized it with his exaltation of America as a "shining city on a hill" in the 1980s). Winthrop did not write this text as an American, but as a Puritan. Any exceptionalism he intimated was that the stakes of their venture were so exceptionally high that if they blew it, he and his fellow Puritan émigrés would be made a shameful "story and a byword through the world," and would see their "prayers to be turned into Cursses upon us." And any exceptionalism he articulated was based on his vision of a community founded on "meekenes, gentlenes, patience and liberallity." Such a community was to be "knitt more nearly together" in everything they did, every law they enacted, every economic arrangement they hammered out.[11] Winthrop envisioned a form of social organization that valued goodness over greatness, and community over individuality.

More than two hundred years passed before Winthrop's conception of the Puritans' special charge would become refashioned as American exceptionalism. However, other early thinkers stepped in with formulations that helped British Americans carve out an identity for themselves in a land distant from their country of origin, with uncertain futures, as they were pawns and players in the jockeying for supremacy and survival between the worlds of empire. Cotton Mather employed a version of America's special mission as he drafted his magisterial *Magnalia Christi Americana: or, The Ecclesiastical History of New-England, from Its First Planting in the Year 1620, until the Year of Our Lord 1698* (1702), which offered America up to world history as a refuge from the degeneracies of Christianity in Europe, and a chance to start anew. It is the image rattling around in Thomas Paine's consciousness as he drafted *Common Sense* in 1776 to awaken revolutionary-era Americans to the possibility that "We have it in our power to begin the world over again."[12] All are variations on a theme that would reappear time and again in developments in American thought: the struggle for moral identification in America, as Americans, that bridges the gulfs of its diversity while also providing a view of itself in the wider world.

British subjects in early America often had a difficult time distinguishing between the aspirational and the actual dimensions of the world-historic nature of their new land. They often wrestled with the symbolic America they carried with them from home and the realities they encountered in their daily lives. And yet, while they often failed to mark boundaries between their ideas and first-hand experiences of the New World, they were remarkably successful in drawing other kinds of intellectual distinctions between the New World and Old World, between the promise of regeneration and the threat of degeneration, and between God's Word and the babel of "savages."

Chapter 2

America and the Transatlantic
Enlightenment: 1741–1800

The idea that America might have a world-historic mission naturally appealed to colonists struggling to make new lives for themselves in a foreign land. But it also had an ineluctable appeal to eighteenth-century European observers bristling at home under heavy-handed monarchies, profligate aristocracies, a coercive church, and stubbornly calcified customs. Few of them confused America's resource-rich lands with the Elysian Fields. But they thought that if ever there were a place in the world where such a sublime thing could exist, America was it. This providential notion of America gripped John Locke's imagination in the *Second Treatise of Government* (1689). "Thus in the beginning all the World was *America*," Locke proclaimed, casting the New World as England's second Genesis.[1]

Locke's affirmation that "all the World was *America*" performed a double duty. First, it foreshadowed the enormous influence his ideas would exert in eighteenth-century American life. His colonial readers adopted his hopeful empiricism, thus making his assertion that experience could chart a path to human improvement an axiom of American thought. Locke assured them that their Christianity was reasonable and therefore could tolerate the kind of religious difference they had to negotiate in their new land. And he persuaded them that they were endowed with natural rights, which meant that the role of their government was straightforward: to safeguard them.

But "all the World was *America*" does more than augur the dramatic impact his ideas would have on Americans' minds. It also reveals the impact that America had on Europeans' minds.

America played an important role—both as ideal and lived reality—in the imaginations of eighteenth-century European thinkers seeking enlightenment. It ushered in a startling new picture of the natural world and all the living things upon it. It offered alluring and disturbing evidence that would catalyze an effort to raze all canons of established knowledge and to replace them with ideas unheard of in world history.

British Americans contributed to Enlightenment thought not so much by inventing new ideas about human nature, the natural world, history, and government, but by testing and reformulating ideas that in eighteenth-century Europe could only be theorized. That is not to say that America was simply a laboratory for European ideas. It became much more than that, especially during, and in the years following, the American Revolution. The very fact of its existence as a nation founded on ideals rather than hereditary claims made it both a participant in and a source of the dramatic shift in Western thought known as the Enlightenment.

The Transatlantic Republic of Letters

Ideas are immaterial, but they need material structures to make people aware of them. The sprawling, buzzing, messy transatlantic "republic of letters" provided those structures, or rather that infrastructure, for an unprecedented global traffic of ideas. The republic of letters was a vast network of feverish intellectual activity—theorizing, collecting, examining, testing, producing, disseminating, and either accepting, modifying, or skewering new understandings of human nature and the world. It was inhabited by scholars and independent thinkers, theorists and empiricists, publishing houses and salons, academies and universities. Along the republic of letters' crooked routes traveled texts, specimens, artwork, and inventions between capitals, provinces, and remote locations across the globe. This remarkable new form of intellectual community connected James Madison in Montpelier to Samuel von Pufendorf in Lund, Benjamin Rush in Philadelphia to Mary Wollstonecraft in London, Judith Sargent Murray in Gloucester to Nicolas de Condorcet in Paris, and Voltaire to his various, though temporary, safe havens in Brussels, Cirey-sur-Blaise, Potsdam, and Geneva. But the republic of letters was more than a geographical network. It was also a temporal one, helping to bring classical Athens and Rome into the mindscapes of eighteenth-century American and European philosophers, political theorists, and poets.

Nevertheless, the circulation of Enlightenment ideas did not produce a smooth sameness across the globe. There were differences, mostly national, that gave the Enlightenment different inflections in France, Germany, Italy, England, Scotland, and the British colonies. The particularities multiply when looking beyond the transatlantic republic of letters to the wider networks of global trade, bringing "enlightened" ideas and systems of thought to and from China, India, the Hispanophone world, and beyond.

What gave the Enlightenment ideas in America their distinct form, and one strikingly different from the Enlightenment in France, in particular, is that America's foremost thinkers were not hostile to religion. Indeed, many were friendly to religion if not deeply religious themselves. The Great Awakening of the 1740s helped pave the way for renewed spiritual commitments, and though the founders did not share in its missionary zeal, they tried to reconcile the head and the heart. "Sensibility" or "moral sense" was a keyword for them, which represented the blending of the two. Indeed, they had drawn the notion of a "moral sense" from the works of Scottish Common Sense philosophers, Thomas Reid especially, who exerted a powerful influence on American readers. The Scottish philosophers lived in the provinces of empire and came from Reformed Christian traditions, so their perspectives harmonized nicely with Americans' experience.

In this regard, there is a world of difference between John Adams, Benjamin Rush, and Judith Sargent Murray and a thinker like Denis Diderot. "Everything," Diderot wrote in his *Encyclopédie* (1772), "must be examined, everything must be shaken up, without exception and without circumspection"— and his American counterparts agreed.[2] They just did not agree that doing so meant that all forms of religion must be shaken so hard that their necks snapped or, worse, that the guillotine's blade separated their heads from their bodies.

Even Thomas Jefferson had a soft spot in his heart for rational Christianity. Though he proposed a "wall of separation between Church and State" and his Federalist critics castigated him for being a "howling Atheist," he maintained a lifelong interest in religion and sought to ensure that freedom of religion would be a foundational principle of the new nation.[3] Jefferson's problem was not with religion or Christianity as such, but rather with people's reliance on miracles and mysticism instead of morality. Jefferson was so interested in considering what aspects of Jesus's life and teaching were still relevant to enlightened moderns that he tasked himself with rereading the New Testament to reintroduce himself to a human (not divine) Jesus he could believe in. Jefferson took a penknife or razor and some glue to the New Testament, cut out all of the passages he found objectionable, reordered parts of the Gospels to create a more coherent portrait of Jesus as a great moral exemplar, and titled it *The Life and Morals of Jesus of Nazareth* (1820).

In the busy traffic of the republic of letters flowed new ideas about human intelligence, agency, and self-sovereignty; the ideal form of government; historical progress; and a firm belief that the unknown world was eminently knowable. This optimism helped embolden many observers to imagine that American independence was not an accident of empire, but rather a fulfillment of providence. George Washington made this providentialism clear in his

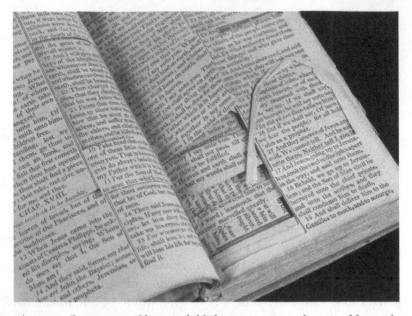

Thomas Jefferson created his own bible by cutting out and reassembling only those passages of the New Testament that he believed could stand at the bar of the enlightened mind. The result, *The Life and Morals of Jesus of Nazareth, Extracted Textually from the Gospels in Greek, Latin, French & English* (1820), demonstrates that powerful new ideas can come in the form of selective erasure of old ones. *Division of Political History, National Museum of American History, Smithsonian Institution*

"Circular to the States" of 1783. "The foundation of our Empire," Washington contended,

> was not laid in the gloomy age of Ignorance and Superstition, but at an Epocha when the rights of mankind were better understood and more clearly defined, than at any former period, the researches of the human mind, after social happiness, have been carried to a great extent, the Treasures of knowledge, acquired by the labours of Philosophers, Sages and Legislatures, through a long succession of years, are laid open for our use, and their

collected wisdom may be happily applied in the Establishment of our forms of Government.[4]

This circular may sound like a love letter to his fellow countrymen and women, but it was actually a stern warning, much like John Winthrop's 150 years earlier: "At this auspicious period, the United States came into existence as a Nation, and if their Citizens should not be completely free and happy, the fault will be intirely their own."[5]

The Enlightened Eye and Its Blind Spots

Enlightenment thinkers put a heavy premium on the eye. They associated vision with insight, discernment, understanding, and even omniscience. The Scottish philosopher Thomas Reid believed that "Of all the faculties called the five senses, sight is without doubt the noblest," while Locke maintained that sight was "the most comprehensive of all our Senses."[6] The English social theorist Jeremy Bentham took this Enlightenment glorification of the eye to new heights by developing his "panopticon" as a building plan for penitentiaries, schools, and asylums. His design put a circular structure in the center of the building so that an administrator could see all of his wards around the perimeter, but the wards were not able to see him, thus disciplining them with the specter of constant surveillance. A triumph of the enlightened eye over the forces of darkness, the panopticon was Bentham's "new mode of obtaining power of mind over mind, in a quantity hitherto without example."[7]

The Enlightenment quest for a view of the world unobstructed by false prejudices propelled a veritable building boom of new institutions of learning to foster the acquisition and dissemination of knowledge in mid to late eighteenth-century America. In 1731, Benjamin Franklin founded the Library Company of Philadelphia so that he and his friends could more easily share books. Twelve years later in 1743, he helped found the American Philosophical

The Phantasmagoria, like the Panopticon, was an Enlightenment-era invention. Phantasmagorias were a popular form of entertainment that relied on hidden, specially constructed "magic" lanterns and mirrors to project images of apparitions, skeletons, and demons onto plumes of smoke (hence "smoke and mirrors"). Though audiences yelped, screamed, and clapped for the terrifying bogeys, the aim of these shows was not to mystify or enchant but rather to debunk popular belief in a spectral realm. *Frontispiece, Memoires recreatifs, scientifiques et anecdotiques du physician-aeronaute, vol. 1, E. G. Robertson (Paris, 1831), University of Wisconsin–Madison, Special Collections*

Society in Philadelphia, the first learned society in the colonies. John Adams, Samuel Adams, and John Hancock founded the American Academy of Arts and Sciences in 1780 with the pledge "to cultivate every art and science which may tend to advance the interest, honor, dignity, and happiness of a free, independent, and virtuous people." In the 1750s, a wave of scientific societies, literary salons, conversation clubs, subscription libraries, and study circles began cropping up all over American urban centers. Driving this flurry of intellectual foundings was the belief that open inquiry, reasoned debate, careful experimentation, and sociability are the marks of an enlightened society. Being enlightened meant valuing the free play of the mind, to be sure. But it also meant recognizing the importance of intellectual structures and training to cultivate, as Franklin's Junto put it, "Reason's eye."[8]

The goal for educated Americans was not simply to strive for enlightenment, but also to pass that enlightenment down to future generations. Fueled by this impulse, educators established a number of colleges in quick succession, including the College of Philadelphia (later renamed the University of Pennsylvania) in 1740, the College of New Jersey (later renamed Princeton University) in 1746, King's College (later renamed Columbia University) in 1754, Dartmouth College in 1769, the University of Georgia in 1785, the University of North Carolina in 1789, and the University of South Carolina in 1801. Harvard, founded in 1636, was the first institution of higher learning in America, and in 1643 beat all of its future rivals by choosing for its seal a word they likely would have wanted for their own institutions: "Veritas" (Truth). All of these institutions similarly sought to announce to young men that they could instill in them reason, virtue, and even wisdom. Princeton seized on "Leges sine moribus vanae" (Laws without morals are useless), the University of South Carolina promised that "Emollit Mores Nec Sinit Esse Feros" (Learning humanizes character and does not permit it to be cruel), and King's College had the clever idea to work with the Enlightenment's proud ocularcentrism while using the language of the Psalms: "In lumine Tuo videbimus lumen" (In thy light shall we see light).

Immanuel Kant identified this inquisitive impulse of the Enlightenment as "Sapere Aude!" (Dare to know).[9] That audacious intellectual hunger and drive inspired many young American women who were barred from all of these homosocial bastions of learning. With the exception of Moravian College in Bethlehem, Pennsylvania, which was founded in 1742, institutions of higher learning for women did not begin to appear until the mid-nineteenth century. However, the push for female enlightenment led to the founding of nearly four hundred female academies and seminaries between 1780 and 1830. One of those was Milcah

Martha Moore's school for girls in Philadelphia, where she provided students with a commonplace book she had compiled for their instruction: *Miscellanies, moral and instructive, in prose and verse: collected from various authors, for the use of schools, and improvement of young persons of both sexes* (1787). As with Jefferson's Bible, Moore had to cut and paste fragments of wisdom from predominantly male authors to help establish what, by her own lights, were convincing examples of the way Christian reasoning and contemplation could establish an "empire in the mind" of her pupils. She too likened enlightenment to seeing anew with a well-trained eye: "active thought unseals my eye."[10]

Despite Enlightenment thinkers' passion for comprehensive vision, many of their intellectual and moral viewpoints were obstructed by some rather profound blind spots, even for their own time. That women had to work so hard to have access to a rigorous education reveals one of the ways in which Enlightenment thought was blinkered. Men could go to colleges and participate in one of many intellectual societies, and they had outlets for their education in ministry, the law, medicine, and public life more broadly. Women did not. Nor did they have many male Enlightenment thinkers giving them a hand as they sought to have these opportunities. Scottish philosopher Lord Kames could imagine a new social order, but not new possibilities for women in it: "cultivation of the female mind, is not of great importance in a republic."[11] Montesquieu and Condorcet could fathom that an enlightened civic government could have salutary implications for women's private lives, but they never imagined that women's activities could or should extend into the public sphere. There were exceptions, like John Locke, who offered glimmerings of hope for his female audiences. For them, reading Locke's *Two Treatises of Government* could feel bracing and enlivening, like alpine winds rushing over their minds. Marriage, Locke maintained, was not the dominion of a lord over his subject but rather "a voluntary Compact between Man and Woman."[12] But others still revealed that women were largely afterthoughts of enlightened inquiry. Even in his effort to endorse female independence,

James Otis asked, "Are not women born as free as men?" ironically confessing that *men* were really what Enlightenment thinkers had in mind when they exalted "man."[13]

American women not content to let Enlightenment generalizations about "man" be a cover for a very specific demographic had to work hard to try to remove the gendered blinders of Enlightenment thought. Poet, playwright, and essayist Judith Sargent Murray stepped onto the (male) public stage with her challenge to male privilege of the Enlightenment in her essay "On the Equality of the Sexes" (1790). She argued that any differences between men and women were the result not of the human condition but rather of the condition women were forced into by Western culture. Extending the logic of Locke's empiricism, Murray contended that anything experience does to make us who we are can also be undone by new experiences, including any real or perceived discrepancies between the male and female intellect. Murray plumbed ancient texts for examples of female intelligence and power: Athena and Minerva—the Greek and Roman goddesses of wisdom—were the favorites. But she had to work equally hard to keep them as moral and intellectual models for women rather than letting them become mascots for their fathers' and husbands' colleges and clubs. Denying women their independence was unbecoming a truly enlightened republic, Murray contended, and she even dared to envision a future "female Washington" should her fellow male thinkers in the transatlantic republic of letters step out from the dark shadows cast by the light of their Enlightenment.[14]

The universalisms of Enlightenment thought proved deceptive when it came to women and also, especially, when it came to race. A common path for Enlightenment ideas was to meet up with the social justice commitments of Quakers or strands of a liberalizing Protestantism to produce the growing antislavery movement in the northern Atlantic world.

But Enlightenment ideas also took another path, which sent them back to familiar ways of viewing social worlds and providing new justifications for them. For thinkers along that second path, the

Samuel Jennings's painting *Liberty Displaying the Arts and Sciences, Or The Genius of America Encouraging the Emancipation of Blacks* (1792) depicts the figure of Liberty, surrounded by the accoutrements of enlightened knowledge, with the severed chains of freed blacks at her feet. This is the first known painting by an American artist to advocate for the abolition of slavery. *Library Company of Philadelphia*

latest Enlightenment science proved that the differences between the races are as clear as black and white. Whether enlightened Americans lived in the North or South tended to make a big difference, though not a determinative one, in the way they absorbed Enlightenment views of race. Nonslaveholders and even many slaveholders in the North and Mid-Atlantic states saw the findings of Enlightenment racial science as inconsonant with slavery, while for those in the South and the British West Indies, it confirmed the permanent, immutable differences between the races.

Jefferson's *Notes on the State of Virginia* (1781) demonstrates how his enlightened anthropology looked for escape clauses in its claims for a common humanity when it came to nonwhites. Jefferson thought that Africans and African Americans had less body hair than do white Americans. They secreted a foul-smelling odor. They could tolerate heat better but cold worse than whites. They required less sleep. None of these claims would have been particularly objectionable to enlightened antislavery advocates. But when he moved on to issues of blacks' intelligence and their capacity for freedom, abolitionists drew the line. "In memory [blacks] are equal to the whites; in reason much inferior, as I think one could scarcely be found capable of tracing and comprehending the investigations of Euclid." Jefferson's careful investigations (thanks to living among the six hundred African Americans he owned over the course of his life) demonstrated that their imagination proved "dull, tasteless, and anomalous." But when he considered his racial distinctions from the vantage point of a reasonable and fair Creator—the only kind he could possibly believe in—he confessed nagging doubts about his scientific defense of chattel slavery and whether history would be on his side: "I tremble for my country when I reflect that God is just: that his justice cannot sleep for ever: that considering numbers, nature and natural means only, a revolution of the wheel of fortune, an exchange of situation, is among possible events: that it may become probable by supernatural interference!"[15]

Generations of historians have tried to make sense of this claim. Did it reveal a deep fissure that threatened to shatter his Enlightenment framework? Or was it just a random thought that enabled the framework to stay firmly in place? Jefferson did not defend slavery, though he remained a slaveholder until his death. And so new generations of historians will keep asking these questions. But no matter what they conclude, they will no doubt agree that Jefferson provided an authoritative framework and conceptual language for marking racial difference, which would justify the evils he thought unfortunate and hoped were remediable.

Jefferson drafted these words while an army of slaves served his every physical need—an indication that racial oppression was not simply a subject of late eighteenth-century intellectual inquiry but rather provided its material foundation. Nowhere is this connection between racial oppression and intellectual production more conspicuous than in early American universities and colleges themselves. Much like Jefferson, who penned paeans to freedom while he had a workforce of slaves, early American universities were not only sites of Enlightenment race science but also the beneficiaries of racial oppression. Without exception, every American college was built on Native Americans' dispossessed lands. Their connections to slavery varied in scope and kind, but none of them was exempt. Enslaved African Americans helped build many college campuses; in the case of the University of Virginia, they were the sole workforce. Many colleges received large endowments from slave merchants to purchase real estate to build new university campuses, as well as fund professorships. Others, such as Georgetown University, founded in 1789 by John Carroll, the first Catholic bishop in the United States, were able to pass along their funding drawn from the slave economy to students by making enrollment tuition-free. Others heavily recruited children of wealthy slave owners because the children could be cultivated as future trustees.

However, slavery was not just behind the scenes of university knowledge production; it was also an overt presence on early American college campuses. At most colleges, the remuneration for the president came in the form of an annual income and slaves. Some presidents even brought their personal slaves with them. Harvard president Increase Mather (1692–1701) brought an enslaved man given to him by his son Cotton to tend to daily chores. So when Harvard president Benjamin Wadsworth (1725–37) decided to bring his slave Titus with him and to purchase a new "Negro Wench" to join him, he was simply upholding a Harvard tradition.[16]

Many colleges owned slaves who cared for the grounds of campuses and waited on professors and students alike. Students often brought their own personal slaves with them; in 1754 a number of students at the College of William and Mary paid for additional housing so they could bring their human chattel along to serve them while they studied. Even death did not release African Americans from serving the university. Anatomical dissection was a path to discovering the Enlightenment's desire to understand the body and boosted the prestige of medical colleges that could provide post-mortem dissections; the easiest and cheapest bodies to acquire were those of blacks and poor whites. In time, antislavery advocacy would make its way onto American college campuses, but not enough to fully extricate most of them from connections to slavery until after the Civil War.

The most vivid exemplar of the blinkered brilliance of the Enlightenment's enthusiasm for human potential was Benjamin Franklin. Franklin is remembered as the towering figure of the Enlightenment in America because he embodied so many of the traits future readers would find inspiring. As if to testify to the range of human capacity he so exalted, Franklin himself was a printer, ambassador, writer, philanthropist, and experimental scientist. As a publisher and a thinker, he was attentive to the incorporeal dimension of ideas, as well as material ones. He was a master of speculative inquiry and empirical analysis, and was a wellspring of jovial curiosity about his world. He started intellectual institutions founded on the idea of useful knowledge. And when he noticed that other useful things were missing from his world, he envisioned them and gave them material form. Franklin invented swimming fins as an eleven-year-old in 1717, and the lightning rod and an improved urinary catheter in 1752. In 1762, he produced the world's first odometer, and in 1768–69 identified and named the Gulf Stream. And as if to offer a tribute to the Enlightenment's exaltation of the eye with its powers of dispassionate observation, Franklin invented bifocals ("double spectacles" as he referred to them) in 1784. He wanted to conquer the effects of aging to make his "eyes as useful to me as ever they were."[17]

But of all of Franklin's intellectual projects, the one he perfected the most was himself. Franklin both championed and embodied the Enlightenment's premium on human plasticity and improvement. Having come from a modest family of soap and candlemakers, he did not want to wait for a higher power to bestow him with good fortune or condemn him to a life of modest means. So he took his life into his own hands. In his *Autobiography* (1791), he explained his "bold and arduous project of arriving at *moral perfection*," suggesting these were technologies of the self any reader could employ.[18] Perfection meant turning the twelve virtues he wanted to cultivate into second nature: temperance, silence, order, resolution, frugality, industry, sincerity, justice, moderation, cleanliness, tranquility, and chastity. When a Quaker friend gently reminded him that he had left out one virtue he could use a little more of—humility—Franklin conceded and added it to the list to bring it up to thirteen.

Franklin had his glorious vision of self-perfection and a perfectable world, and he had his bifocals to help him see grand achievements in the distant future, as well as practical steps to realize them up close. But as a quintessential Enlightenment figure, he too had his social blind spots. In addition to his knack for industriousness and regimentation, he had his common-law wife, Deborah, to take care of their two children and his illegitimate son; a devoted sister, Jane, who, though an impoverished mother of twelve, served as her elder brother's scribe, family recordkeeper, and personal soap maker; and household slaves who tended to his earthly needs so that he could devote his time to cultivating his virtues. (He eventually manumitted his slaves and late in life became an abolitionist.) But while he extolled independence, he had a virtual staff of loved ones and subordinates to help him cultivate his self-reliance. Franklin, much like many of the other brilliant but nevertheless all-too-human *philosophes* of the transatlantic Enlightenment, was blind to the social and economic conditions that made his quest for Enlightenment possible.

Revolutionary Republicanism

Enlightenment ideals animated the trinity of late eighteenth-century political revolutions in the British colonies, France, and Haiti. In each setting, former supplicants to monarchs, feudalism, and empire razed and remade their country's entire political, economic, and legal topography, and with it, the course of world history. None were without enormous human costs, or without evidence that while human ingenuity and collective will can lead to innovations such as the Declaration of Independence (1776), they can also produce disturbing inventions such as the guillotine (in France in 1789). Although the American Revolution cannot exclusively claim to have put Enlightenment ideals into practice, it can claim to have been the first to try to do so. The prospect that a modern nation could be founded on a shared set of ideas, rather than a shared *Volk*, history, language, or religion (which America had none of), seemed too impossible to achieve and sustain for many observers at the time, including some of the American revolutionaries themselves. Thus, before waging a fearsome war over the future of the colonies, a dramatic intellectual transformation had to occur first. As John Adams later put it: "The Revolution was effected before the war commenced. The Revolution was in the minds and hearts of the people."[19]

Enlightenment thinking circulated through all of the highways and byways of the transatlantic republic of letters, catalyzing a radically new view of a progressive universe, and with it, the prospect that the future of humankind could look better than its past. It was crucial to revolutionary-era literate Americans, but it required another intellectual concept to turn its ideals into an actual model of a government and its people. "Liberty" was the key term, but also a hazy one. It was the invocation of the word "republican" that helped give colonists' angry grievances and vague aspirations their radical form. What they meant by "republican" seems straightforward by modern standards, even indubitable. But for that time, it seemed both outrageous and utopian: namely, a government for the *res publica* (literally a "public matter" or "public affair," which in eighteenth-century political thought became identified as "the public good"). What kind of government fosters and defends a public good? The "republican" answer was a government that is run by its citizens rather than one headed by a hereditary king.

Republicanism had to travel far and wide before making its entrance into the textual marketplace and then into the minds of revolutionary Americans. They picked it up and reformulated it from the English-Dissenting tradition, which had picked it up and reformulated it from Renaissance political thought, which in turn had picked it up from (or rather imagined how it was in) antiquity. When American revolutionaries came into contact with republican discourses, they did not imagine themselves working with centuries of intellectual adaptations, accretions, and deletions. Rather, they thought themselves directly—and forcefully—into the world of Aristotle, Polybius, Cicero, and Tacitus. They imagined a classical past as a guide to a future America, in which participatory government drew its strength and stability from an independent, virtuous citizenry of equals. Privileges of birth and markers of rank had no place in such a body politic. Distinction was welcome, but only a distinction of merit.

The classical world invoked in republican rhetoric was alive in the colonists' everyday interactions, framing their political apprehensions and aspirations accordingly. As John Adams later put it, "When I read them I seem to be only reading the History of my own Times and my own Life."[20] Women were especially resourceful in repurposing republicanism to fit their current needs. They inhabited a new world of the republican mother who fulfilled her public obligation to the *res publica* by privately distilling and safeguarding virtue in her husband and children. Literate revolutionary-era Americans did not encounter corrupt British imperial administrators so much as experience them as examples of the sort of immoderation described in *Cato's Letters* (1723).

The temptation to backslide and put private interests ahead of the collective welfare awakened revolutionaries' inner Cicero, who whispered reminders about the ennobling power of virtue directly into their consciences. Voicing one's opinion in the newspaper required Sallust and Tacitus as models for a plain style of republican persuasion, as well as a classical figure to provide the appropriate pseudonym. And whenever George III revealed himself to be utterly unmoved by his colonists' pleas, they had Polybius affirming the necessity of mixed government. The classical world provided both a template for good governance and a warning about what would happen if public virtue flagged. As political thinker Hannah Arendt would put it: "Without the classical example . . . none of the men of the revolutions on either side of the Atlantic would have possessed the courage for what then turned out to be unprecedented action."[21]

Thomas Paine and the War of Ideas

The ideas of the Enlightenment clearly energized a new faith in human will, ingenuity, and capacity for self-sovereignty. But revolution? Even the most promising ideas cannot capture historical actors' imaginations enough to thrust them into war without the right conditions on the ground. And so it was in eighteenth-century America. A progression of developments—some the result of chance or contingency, others the result of shortsightedness—made notions of popular sovereignty and constitutionalism in accordance with natural rights seem plausible.

Over the course of the eighteenth century, socioeconomic and demographic transformations altered the way colonists made sense of themselves on the edges of the British Empire. Increasing immigration intensified demands for new lands to settle. Economic forces led the colonies' wealth to become concentrated in fewer and fewer hands, thus dramatically intensifying social and economic stratification among whites. As the diversity of population and stratification grew, so too did forms of social differentiation, causing a gap between colonists' traditional modes of understanding the world and the dizzying changes around them. The French and Indian War added upheaval to the colonies, but what seemed worse from their perspective was the British response to it. To cover the costs of war and imperial expansion, Great Britain instituted a number of measures that raised tensions with colonists. First came the Proclamation Line of 1763, then the Currency Act of 1764, then the Sugar Act of 1764, and then the Stamp Act of 1765, each one more punishing than the one before. The Boston Massacre of 1770 sparked a crisis, but the Tea Act of 1773 and the Coercive Acts of 1774 put agitated colonists over the edge. Suddenly revolutionary ideas of self-sovereignty, which had been circulating in books, broadsides, and newspapers for years, took on a new urgency. Republicanism pushed them to recognize that they were not the beneficiaries of British imperialism but rather its victims.

But amid all that flurry of print electrifying the colonists, one pamphlet truly awakened them to the prospect that their time to claim independence was now: Thomas Paine's *Common Sense* (1776). World-changing texts achieve their effectiveness through a collaboration of the author's powerful ideas, the right language to express them, and historical circumstance. This helps explain how Thomas Paine set heated colonists ablaze with republican righteousness in January 1776, when *Common Sense* first appeared, and why it needed to go through twenty-five editions in that same year alone. Paine had arrived in America from England just thirteen months earlier, a debt-ridden corset maker with a failing second marriage. Paine was essentially homeless, his only anchor to the world at that time his passionate belief in the evils of monarchy and the promise of liberty and equality for the common man.

To call *Common Sense* an "Enlightenment" text does not quite do justice to its rhetorical and intellectual innovations, which help to show why this text in that time and place had the convulsive power to break history in two. He published it anonymously, which was not uncommon for the time, though most authors preferred pseudonyms to anonyms. (Some of John Adams's friends thought he was its secret author, which partly flattered him because of the sheer force of its ideas and partly offended him because they were expressed in such a vulgar manner. Paine had called King George the "Royal Brute of Britain" but realized that was too complimentary because "even brutes do not devour their young.")[22]

Paine exchanged Latin words for biblical passages, pretense for unsparing candor and sincerity, and the language of learned elites for the expressions and rhetorical forms of common people. Instead of speaking to his audiences from a voice on high, as so many other Enlightenment-era writers did, he voiced his claims from the vantage point of one down low, expressing what it felt like to be pinned to the ground by the heel of a tyrant. In a typically enlightened fashion, he laid out general arguments about the "sinfulness" of monarchy, but he particularized each and every one to the American situation, and then generalized again, giving the fight for independence a world-historical grandeur: "The cause of America is in a great measure the cause of all mankind."[23] He found a voice of "public opinion" among competing factions that did not exist prior to, but was instantiated in, the process of readers taking in his rhetoric. He implored them that the time to act is *now*, before the forces of history pull away from them. "We have it in our power to begin the world over again" were the right words at the right time. They confirmed to British colonials that they were the virtuous, independent community of equals whom the republicans of antiquity had in mind, and that the colonists had Providence on their side. In all, the enthralling lucidity of Paine's prose and the power of his ideas made dreams of independence appear eminently possible.

Looking at the American Revolution through the lens of intellectual history helps draw out the importance of ideas for motivating colonists to take up arms and for giving them a vision of the new way of life for which they were fighting. "Enlightened" and "republican" ideas were central to the drama, as they helped colonists envision a different course than the one they were on, gave motivation that they could effect that change, and provided explanations of what was happening to them during and after the fighting. Making a claim for the causal force of ideas is always a little risky. But in the case of the American Revolution, it is unassailable. British Americans had to believe they had "it in [their] power to begin the world over again" in order to make the effort and take huge risks to try to do so. No doubt, impulsiveness and not a small amount of irrationality are involved in any war, especially a civil war like this one. But in the case of the American Revolution, a prime factor in the causes of the war and the course of a new nation thereafter was the power of ideas. Early Americans needed to think they could make the world anew before attempting to do just that.

Chapter 3

From Republican to Romantic: 1800–1850

In the early years of the republic, as Americans built a new nation, the Enlightenment's intellectual commitments were neither fully realized nor forgotten. "Reason" and "virtue" still gripped the imagination of American political figures, clergy, writers, and their publics. But rapid population growth, westward expansion, urbanization, and industrialization, along with political experiments (and failures) in democracy abroad, put intense pressure on American Enlightenment ideas. The desire for the enlightened republican vision of a government of independent landowners ensured that white freedom would continue to be predicated on black exploitation and Native Americans' dispossession of their ancestral lands and their ways of life.

While few professed to be able to read the mind of God, many vocal proponents of westward expansion were convinced that his desire for white Christendom's transcontinental destiny was manifest. Improvements to technology and the market revolution helped provide critical infrastructure for the new nation, but they also caused many observers to worry that technological and economic advances were outpacing human development and threatening individual autonomy. Nevertheless, those same critics made use of the communications revolution to spread their Romantic visions of alternative paths. Republican ideals fused with new Romantic sensibilities in response to the changing political and social conditions of the early republic.

All of these dramatic changes transformed the ways Americans thought. What antebellum Americans learned from making a new world was that human beings did indeed have it within their power to make, remake, or even destroy worlds. What persisted was a frame of mind with an emboldened sense of human agency and power but also one frightfully aware of the impermanence and instability of their new nation. The desire to remake worlds can be seen in the flurry of evangelical revivals of the Second Great Awakening; utopian experiments including Brook Farm, Oneida, and Ceresco; and reform movements, such as antislavery, prison reform, temperance, and women's rights. But the discomfort with too dramatic a change in customary ways of life helps explain the limits of their influence and, in some cases, their failures.

The most reliable commentators on a period are often those who lived through its changes, and this is especially true when that commentator is Ralph Waldo Emerson. It was as if Emerson had a divining rod to the inner yearnings, worries, and inconsistencies of antebellum Americans' "modern mind." He noted that it "believed that the nation existed for the individual. . . . This idea, roughly written in revolutions and national movements, in the mind of the philosopher had far more precision." America produced a "mind [that] had become aware of itself" and keenly aware of warring impulses of "intellect and affection." A young republic in its gangly adolescence, America during the first half of the nineteenth century produced a generation of "young men [who] were born with knives in their brain, a tendency to introversion, dissection, anatomizing of motives."[1] Emerson, his Transcendentalist coconspirators, and many other critical thinkers of the day showed just what was possible—but also what was not—when enough Americans put their mental cutlery to work to make a new world consonant with its founding ideals.

Made in America, 1.0

The notion of a new nation founded on ideals of its own choosing inspired the French-born American writer J. Hector St. John de Crèvecœur's *Letters from an American Farmer* (1782). In it he posed the memorable question: "What then is the American, this new man?" Crèvecœur thought the answer was both clear and compelling: "He is an American, who leaving behind him all his ancient prejudices and manners, receives new ones from the new mode of life he has embraced, the new government he obeys, and the new rank he holds."[2] In the decades to come, however, American commentators would wrestle with what it meant to leave behind *all* of their inheritances from and intellectual affiliations with Europe, and continue to question just what exactly being "American" even meant.

Well into the nineteenth century it was clear that the Revolutionary War had ruptured America's political ties to the king but not its cultural bonds with England and continental Europe. Even with the considerable expansion of domestic manufacturing in the early republic, Americans who could afford imported consumer goods typically preferred them over those made in America. Pocket watches and candelabras from France; blue and white earthenware from Delft; decorative prints from Bavaria; and chintzes, crockery, and cosmetics from England were all the rage. The origin of the cultural good, often more than the good itself, signified refinement. Elite American children learned to play Mozart and Haydn on their fortepianos imported from Vienna, and practiced good penmanship writing passages from Coleridge and Byron excerpted in American periodicals. But of all the foreign goods in circulation, books were by far the most treasured. South Carolinians, for example, were more likely to read Friedrich Schiller's play *Wilhelm Tell* (1804), which used the Swiss struggle for independence from the

Habsburg Empire as a parable for the American Revolution, than *The History of the American Revolution* (1789), written by their own native son David Ramsay. Few educated Americans in the early republic questioned the axiom that cultivation (what by the 1840s would be called "culture") came from Europe. Even fewer noticed the inconsonance between their criticisms of European decadence and degeneracy and their own heavy reliance on Europe's cultural and intellectual wares.

During the early republic, Americans' consternation over the perceived absence of a native culture fostered efforts to build new intellectual institutions that could cultivate a liberated intellect and habits befitting a politically liberated people. One of the most important initiatives was spearheaded by the Connecticut educator Noah Webster, who had started his career as a schoolteacher in 1778, witnessing firsthand the impediments to educating a citizenry for a republic. His experiences led him to the conclusion that language was as essential for shaping a distinct American identity as was literacy for supporting a fledgling democracy. Troubled that Americans' language was wholly derivative of the English spoken and written in Britain, Webster set out to give Americans an English of their own. "*Language*," he declared, "as well as government should be national. . . . America should have her *own* distinct from all the world."[3] He regarded British English as the product of a decaying civilization, of a Europe "grown old in folly, corruption, and tyranny," and thus thought it was imperative to found a national language.[4]

With this urgency in mind, Webster produced his "bluebacked" *Spelling Book* in 1783, which phonetically simplified and standardized spellings, quickly becoming the authority on American English. With the success of his speller (which sold one and a half million copies and was reprinted fifty times between 1783 and 1801 alone), he set out to further his cause by compiling the first dictionary of American English, *An American Dictionary of the English Language* (1828), to both give new authority to everyday words and set limits on the language of the new nation. Webster regarded it an "honor" (not "honour") to "labor" (not "labour") in the service of American "civilization" (not "civilisation"), while granting himself the "license" (not "licence") to include new American words such as "chowder" and "squash." He clearly wanted to accentuate the difference between the health and vitality of the new American republic and the degeneracy of the Europe it left behind, so he even coined a new word to do so: "demoralize," meaning "to corrupt or undermine the morals of; to destroy or lessen the effect of moral principles on; to render corrupt in morals."[5]

The founding of the Library of Congress is another example of an early effort to cultivate a distinctly American intellect and culture. Initially established in 1800, the library provided resources for the country's legislators. It started out in the north wing of the US Capitol as a modest collection of 740 volumes and three maps. But the library expanded quickly, thanks in part to the vision of Thomas Jefferson. Jefferson was certain that he could not "live without books," and he believed that the new nation could not either.[6] While he was president of the United States, from 1801 to 1809, he facilitated the expansion of the library to become a national library—a resource for all Americans. After the British army invaded Washington, DC, and burned the Capitol in the War of 1812, Jefferson sold his personal collection of more than 6,000 books to the library, which was the biggest collection in America at that time. Thanks to its wide range of subjects, from law, economics, and the natural sciences to literature and the arts, including many works in French, German, Latin, and Greek in addition to English, Jefferson's collection helped turn the Library of Congress into an institution for citizens to imagine their role in their young nation and the wider world, as well as one that stood as a monument of America's intellectual aspirations.

Throughout the early republic and well into the nineteenth century, there were continued efforts to foster a national culture that was more befitting of a democracy while also marking the boundaries of a distinctly American identity. As the case of Prussian expatriate Francis Lieber shows, this urgent work fell even to recent American immigrants. Lieber had arrived in Boston in 1827 after having been persecuted for participating in liberal movements in Prussia, and he saw no better testament of his fidelity to the cause of liberal freedoms than to help provide Americans with an intellectual record of their own. He thus gave his new adopted homeland its very own *Encyclopedia Americana* (1829–33), which he modeled on the *Conversations-Lexikon* (1796–1808), later referred to as the *Brockhaus Enzyklopädie,* as way of documenting and cataloging knowledge necessary for a national body. Drawing on the rich tradition of German scholarship, he applied his knowledge and expertise to this Enlightenment enterprise, attempting to catalog, classify, and organize everything about the known (American) world. Thus, Lieber, like so many immigrants to America before and after him, played a vital role in the making of an "American" national culture.

But despite all of these efforts, educated Americans still sought to keep abreast of intellectual developments in Europe. One of them, which proved both influential but also troubling, was German Romanticism, with its exaltation of the idea of the *Volk* (folk), as this caused them additional consternation about living off a culture secondhand. The philosopher Johann Gottfried von Herder provided the most bracing version of this notion when he mingled ideas about *Kultur* (culture) and *Geist* (spirit) to imagine a people knitted together by a common history, language, tradition, and sensibility. Propelled by the rudimentary nations taking shape in France and America, Herder's Romantic impulse emphasized that only an organic *Volksgeist*—not social contracts, not laws, not leaders—could be the basis of a true *Vaterland* (fatherland), which was his preferred term for the modern "nation-state."

Herder's Romantic nationalism was an intoxicating brew. The only problem for his American readers was that their America did not have a *Volk* nurtured by a common *Kultur,* which was expressive of a singular *Geist.* And it certainly was no *Fatherland*—it was nothing other than a contractual arrangement. America was populated with peoples, but not a people, who, with the exception of the Indians, were all transplants from different parts of Europe, each with their own mother tongues, faith traditions, and cultural sensibilities. In fact, there was no substantive "American" anything prior to the creation of a nation by that name and solidified in the drafting of its Declaration of Independence, its early laws, and its formal Constitution. Indeed, that is precisely what made the American experiment seem so extraordinary and filled with promise just a few decades earlier.

With the influx of early Romantic ideas, this notion of national belonging as something one inherits rather than becomes would give some of Herder's early nineteenth-century American readers pause. Without roots in collective memory and tribal bonds knitting the people to each other and to a homeland, was it even possible to be a nation? And if so, what could legitimately serve as the basis for that nation's collective imagination and affections? These were some of the questions that both vexed and energized many American thinkers for the decades to come.

Biblical Science and Liberal Protestantism

Thomas Paine's *Common Sense* broke every record in America's short publishing history. Whereas books typically had press runs of no more than 2,000 copies and pamphlets roughly 1,000, *Common Sense* sold more than 120,000 copies in its first year alone. One of the reasons for its success was that he worked so effectively with biblical references long familiar to colonists and reformulated them as arguments against monarchy. He drew liberally from the Old Testament to show that only "the King of heaven" could be Israel's "proper Sovereign."[7] For Paine, it was simple common sense to see that the Bible showed Americans that monarchical government was ungodly.

But after the revolution, Paine came to doubt that institutionalized Christianity could be a force for freedom in the new republic, and he turned his sights to divesting it of its moral authority in *The Age of Reason; Being an Investigation of True and Fabulous Theology* (1794). "It is from the Bible that man has learned cruelty, rapine, and murder; for the belief of a cruel God makes a cruel man," he argued, using the same fervor with which he had once employed the Bible in the cause of freedom.[8] Here he concluded that the Bible was "more. . . the word of a demon, than the Word of God," and would leave his conscience to its own best moral resources: "My own mind is my own church." Franklin and Jefferson may have privately shared his sentiment that "pure and simple deism" was the best religion for the fledgling republic, but they tried to persuade him not to publish such incendiary claims in a devoutly Christian America.[9] Like *Common Sense*, his *Age of Reason* was a commercial success (though not on the scale of the earlier book), but it was panned by former supporters (Adams described it as the product of a "malignant heart"), and Paine was ostracized for the remainder of his life.[10]

Rather than being a force for loosening the Bible's hold on Americans' minds, *The Age of Reason* inspired a religious counterattack that made Paine's fervor seem restrained. The revolutionary-era lawyer and statesman Elias Boudinot (who was baptized in 1740 by the First Great Awakening Anglican minister George Whitefield) was so appalled with Paine's blasphemy that he wrote a stern rebuke in *The Age of Revelation, or, the Age of Reason Shewn to Be an Age of Infidelity* (1801). It was a commercial flop, but Boudinot was determined to let the Word get the last word. So in 1816 he joined forces with delegates from small biblical societies from all over the country and formed the American Bible Society (ABS). The goal of the ABS was to get scripture into the hands (and hearts) of every American. The ABS used the latest print technologies to scale the production to meet its bold aspirations and built distribution networks into un-settled frontier regions; this ensured that the gospel would expand along every path of western migration. Its efforts paid off hand-somely: from the early republic through the Civil War, the Bible be-came the single most printed, distributed, and read (extensively and intensively) text in American society.

However, to say that the Bible was the single most important text in antebellum American life is not to say that all those Americans agreed on what they were reading. Biblical interpretation varied widely—even wildly—from denomination to denomination, re-gion to region. And some of the most powerful forces parsing those interpretations came not from critics outside the church, like Paine, but from reformers within it.

"Biblical criticism" or "higher criticism," coming mostly out of Germany and England, was one of those forces remaking early nineteenth-century belief. It was a new method of exegesis that relied on the most recent insights of philology, history, and arche-ology to reevaluate the Bible in terms of the new sciences. A di-rect outgrowth of the Enlightenment, biblical criticism appealed to the authority of rationalism as an aid to improving religious belief and practice. One of the strongest impulses at work was the desire to study the Hebrew and Christian scriptures as his-torical texts, to see where they lined up with knowledge of the social contexts from which they came, and to examine the human traces on their production. The aim of biblical criticism was not to undermine the authority of scripture but to use science to distin-guish what Unitarian minister Theodore Parker in 1841 referred to as "the transient and permanent in Christianity."[11]

Many American colleges and seminaries began teaching this new methodology just as theological journals promoted the discoveries unearthed by its approach, which included compelling evidence of inaccurate dating in the Bible, discrepancies between different translations, and multiple authorship of stories thought to be the Word of God.

This method of scriptural interpretation was welcomed most especially by liberal Congregationalists, whose interest was in employing science as a means to loosen the grip of austere forms of Calvinism in order to get to the deeper truths of their faith and to transcend doctrinal differences. In some cases, biblical criticism only reinforced the liberalizing, modern, and rationalist direction in which some American Congregationalist clergy and theologians were already heading. The most important figure in this development was the Congregationalist-turned-Unitarian William Ellery Channing, who, in his sermon "Unitarian Christianity" (1819), pushed for using reason as the arbiter of religious beliefs. "If reason be so dreadfully darkened by the fall, that its most decisive judgments on religion are unworthy of trust," he maintained, "then Christianity, and even natural theology, must be abandoned; for the existence and veracity of God, and the divine original of Christianity, are conclusions of reason, and must stand or fall with it." The application of Enlightenment faith in human reason, he asserted, required getting rid of the "fictions of theologians" such as a wrathful God, the Trinity (which he regarded as "irrational and unscriptural"), and an emphasis on man's depravity rather than goodness.[12] Channing laid out many a "moral argument against Calvinism," asserting that even John Calvin would have found the dour, forbidding, austere religion that sprang up in his name an abomination.[13]

Unitarianism may have pushed the logic of the Enlightenment the furthest, but it was not the only Protestant faith to welcome rationalism and historicism in its approach to religion. Liberal-minded Congregationalists, and in time other Protestants, welcomed Enlightenment notions of human progress and perfectibility as they built what they increasingly referred to as "humane" (i.e., tender, compassionate) social and legal institutions, and ease their own accommodation to the worldly pursuits of the burgeoning market economy and commercialism.

The Making of Transcendentalism

Beginning in the early 1830s, the twin desires to cultivate an intellectual life more expressive of American experience and to bring religion in line with secular knowledge energized a loose circle of thinkers in and around Boston who came to be known as Transcendentalists. This diverse group of liberal theologians, Romantic writers, and social reformers included, among many others, Ralph Waldo Emerson, Margaret Fuller, Henry David Thoreau, Theodore Parker, George Ripley, Elizabet Parker Peabody, and Bronson Alcott. They were a vibrant and unruly group of restless seekers hungry for novelty, eager to break out of their intellectually cramped religious inheritances, desperate to tap into the resplendent particularity of every individual soul, and ever-struggling to find the balance between individual protest and social commitment.

Many Transcendentalists shared concerns that grew out of their backgrounds in Unitarianism. Though they affirmed the Unitarian belief in the human capacity for good, they regarded its heavy emphasis on reason over spirit as a "corpse cold" way of being in the world. Trained as Unitarian ministers, Emerson, Parker, and Ripley took a different tack than the Congregationalist minister and leading light of nineteenth-century liberal theology Horace Bushnell. Though they read the same Bible, biblical criticism, and European Romanticism, the Unitarians typically took these intellectual influences to abandon theology as the prime realm of their intellectual work. Bushnell, however, used them to radically reinvent theology, thereby becoming a unique bridge figure between the Transcendentalists' Romanticism and naturalism on the one hand and Calvinist supernaturalism and acceptance of original sin on the other.

The Transcendentalists welcomed the notion of a transcendent realm of nature, but not a supernatural one, and therefore repudiated even the remaining traces of supernatural explanations in their own

Unitarianism. They rejected the Unitarian belief that the miracles in the New Testament were proof of the divinity of Jesus Christ. Instead, they held that Christian doctrine was true and deserved assent not because it was proven by a few divine parlor tricks eighteen hundred years before, but because it was true self-evidently, universally, and timelessly. Likewise, the Transcendentalist ministers downplayed the unique divinity of Christ, arguing that all people were equally divine. This notion inspired Emerson in 1838 to address Divinity School graduates with the claim that

> Historical Christianity has fallen into the error that corrupts all attempts to communicate religion. As it appears to us, and as it has appeared for ages, it is not the doctrine of the soul, but an exaggeration of the personal, the positive, the ritual. It has dwelt, it dwells, with noxious exaggeration about the *person* of Jesus. The soul knows no persons. It invites every man to expand to the full circle of the universe, and will have no preferences but those of spontaneous love.[14]

The Divinity School repaid Emerson for his blasphemy by banishing him from Harvard for the next thirty years. The Harvard clergy were scandalized to discover that one of their own graduates and a man of the cloth would come in and "admonish" their students "first of all, to go alone; to refuse the good models, even those which are sacred in the imagination of men, and dare to love God without mediator or veil."[15]

Though the central ideas of Transcendentalism come out of Unitarianism, much of its inspiration also comes from trends in European thought. The more literary of the writers gravitated to the beauty and emotional range found in the poetry of the British Romantics, including Thomas Carlyle, William Wordsworth, and Percy Bysshe Shelley. Transcendental social reformers turned to the post-Kantian empiricism of Victor Cousin and to the communitarian ideas of French socialist Charles Fourier for his science of social perfection. Though critical of the traces of pantheism and subjectivism they detected in German philosophy, a number of Transcendentalists nevertheless discovered in Friedrich Heinrich Jacobi and Friedrich Schleiermacher insights on the intuitiveness of religion; in Friedrich Wilhelm Joseph Schelling a philosophy of nature as the artwork of God; and in Johann Wolfgang von Goethe a model of moral self-reliance. Like their European counterparts, the Transcendentalists mined translated sources of Eastern philosophy and mysticism for the qualities they sought in themselves: awe, a sense of wholeness, and enchantment. As Thoreau confessed in *A Week on the Concord and Merrimack Rivers* (1849): "The reading which I love best is the scriptures of the several nations, though it happens that I am better acquainted with those of the Hindoos, the Chinese, and the Persians, than that of the Hebrews.... Give me one of these Bibles and you have silenced me for a while."[16] Thoreau's imagination, like that of his other Transcendentalist friends and coconspirators, traveled far and wide looking for new intellectual sources to guide the American democratic experiment and to inspire a new, liberated personality.

American Transcendentalists were thus very much part of a transnational flurry of Romantic texts and ideas, but to view it as an outpost of European thought would miss how and why they employed foreign intellectual sources and to what end. Like Noah Webster and Francis Lieber before them, the Transcendentalists wanted nothing more than to create an American intellectual voice and vision befitting the experience of the new nation. They were all diehard fans of Goethe, but when the German master praised their America as a land of innocence, sloughed free of encrusted traditions and liberated to know itself and the universe in terms of its own making, he both buoyed them with visions of intellectual liberation and terrified them that their culture was too immature and insubstantial to pull off such a feat.

None was as enlivened and disturbed by the vision of American newness and innocence as Ralph Waldo Emerson. Though celebrated as the thinker who gave form to a distinctly American intellectual tradition, Emerson spent his career drawing attention to its shortcomings. He affirmed that the life of the mind was not only a life well lived but also essential to a vibrant democracy. And yet he worried that the democratic, capitalist forces in American antebellum life worked against the cultivation of the intellectual wealth of the commonwealth so vital to its own well-being. "The American Scholar" (1837), his most concise meditation on the American mind, and one that Oliver Wendell Holmes Jr. exalted as the nation's "intellectual Declaration of Independence," nevertheless contains some of his most potent terms for describing an American mind indifferent to or incapable of sustained, rigorous intellectual engagement.[17] Emerson expressed concern about a "people too busy [for] letters"; a society that thinks of human life in averages and aggregates, as if men were "bugs," "spawn," and "the herd"; and the "sluggish and perverted mind of the multitude," which showed regard only for "exertions of mechanical skill" but no esteem for the reason and revelation wrought by philosophical inquiry and speculation. He describes Americans as caught up in the immediacy of making a living while forgetting what makes life worth living. Emerson warned: "See already the tragic consequence. The mind of this country, taught to aim at low objects, eats upon itself."[18]

Emerson believed that the democratic mind could aim higher only by learning to express itself in terms of its own making. In his estimation, that enterprise meant a new style of thinking organic to and uniquely expressive of the American experience. He longed for an American intellect free from the bullying thoughts of foreign traditions: piety should be reserved for the process of one's own thinking, not the product of another culture's thought. He believed that this achievement was possible only once American intellect ended its "long apprenticeship to the learning of other lands" and stopped feeding on the "remains of foreign harvests."[19] All truths are achieved, not inherited; they are prospective, never retrospective.

a terrible simplicity. It does not need that a
poem should be long. Every word was once
a poem. Every new relation is a new word.
Also, we use defects and deformities to a sacred purpose, so expressing our sense that the
evils of the world are such only to the evil eye.
In the old mythology, mythologists observe,
defects are ascribed to divine natures, as lame-
ness to Vulcan, blindness to Cupid, and the
like, to signify exuberances.

For, as it is dislocation and detachment
from the life of God, that makes things ugly,
the poet, who re-attaches things to nature and
the Whole,—re-attaching even artificial things,
and violations of nature, to nature, by a deeper
insight,—disposes very easily of the most dis-
agreeable facts. Readers of poetry see the
factory-village, and the railway, and fancy that
the poetry of the landscape is broken up by
these; for these works of art are not yet con-
secrated in their reading; but the poet sees
them fall within the great Order not less than
the bee-hive, or the spider's geometrical web.
Nature adopts them very fast into her vital
circles, and the gliding train of cars she loves
like her own. Besides, in a centred mind, it

Herman Melville heavily annotated his personal copy of Emerson's "Poet" in
Essays; Second Series, but not always with words of approval. He feigns shock
at the top of the page: " 'Defects' signify 'exuberances.'—My Dear Sir!" and at
the bottom he asks in exasperation "What does the man mean?" *AC85.M4977.
Zz844e, Houghton Library, Harvard University*

Emerson's vision in "Self-Reliance" of life—not as being, but as ever creatively becoming—retains the power to knock the wind out of its readers as much today as it did when it first appeared in 1841: "Life only avails, not the having lived. Power ceases in the instant of repose; it resides in the moment of transition from a past to a new state, in the shooting of the gulf, in the darting to an aim. This one fact the world hates, that the soul *becomes*; for that for ever degrades the past, turns all riches to poverty, all reputation to a shame, confounds the saint with the rogue, shoves Jesus and Judas equally aside."[20] Emerson called his American intellectual ideal "*Man Thinking*," and he considered him to be a figure capable of embodying this aboriginal power.[21] He was the "plain old Adam, the simple genuine Self" with no history at his back, who enjoys an original relationship with the universe.[22]

All of the Transcendentalists developed their own terms for describing the direct, unmediated, radiant divinity of the self. For Channing that was "likeness to God," for Emerson it was "Oversoul," Walt Whitman called it the "Song of Myself," and Elizabeth Palmer Peabody described it as something for her male colleagues to *avoid*: "ego-theism." Two other favorites common to them all were "Genius" and "conscience." Their paths to that higher self were as diverse as they were. For Lydia Maria Child, the trail led her to campaign for the rights of slaves, Native Americans, and women, while experimenting with different literary forms to make her case. For George Ripley, following the economic depression of the 1840s, it led to the founding of the socialistic community of Brook Farm, based on a model of organic collectivization and flat labor hierarchies, as a corrective to the exploitation in the emergent capitalist economy. And for Henry David Thoreau, tapping into one's higher self meant trying to figure out what a principled life in harmony with nature could look like at Walden Pond, resisting a government that sanctions the moral abomination of slavery, and finding various strategies (such as withholding one's poll tax) to protest against unjust wars.

Altogether, the Transcendentalists took a variety of intellectual, social, and political paths to release the self from outworn beliefs, to free supplicants from exploitation, and to bring American culture into its own. Though they were exceptionally cosmopolitan in their reading and their appreciation of other cultures and ideas, the Transcendentalists were deeply committed to their New England heritage and to a vibrant future for the American republic. The path to this better future, they believed, followed the course of new thinking about the relationship between the individual and God and between independence and obligation.

The Split Screen of the Southern Mind

The movement of ideas rarely respects national borders. In the eighteenth century, the republic of letters fostered a transnational exchange of Enlightenment thought. A century before that, information about the New World and its inhabitants had a profound impact on European thinking and informed the worldviews of those Europeans who crossed the Atlantic to build new lives there. The same is true with nineteenth-century Romanticism. The texts of its major poets, philosophers, and social theorists traversed the English Channel to and from Britain and the countries of Northern Europe, across to America and back again. But over the course of much of the nineteenth century, the traffic of intellectual exchanges did manage to respect one border: the 36°30′ parallel of the United States, set out by the Missouri Compromise in 1820 to demarcate free Northern from Southern slave states.

This is not to say that there were no cross-border intellectual transactions (indeed, white Northerners and white Southerners were reading many of the same texts), but rather that their mental and moral worlds grew steadily apart during the first half of the nineteenth century, and that their competing economic systems had everything to do with it. Between 1774 and 1804, all Northern states gradually abolished slavery as they moved toward an industrialized economy, though the actual emancipation of slaves would prove slow and fitful. In the South, however, slavery increased exponentially (from roughly seven hundred thousand in 1790 to almost four million by the start of the Civil War). The hideous irony of Eli Whitney's cotton gin of 1793 was that instead of decreasing the burdens of human labor on Southern plantations, it unleashed a rapacious demand for slaves as cotton became the nation's most valuable commercial crop during the first half of the nineteenth century, and America's largest foreign export.

As the North and South developed two very different (though interdependent) economic systems, so too did they develop two very different ways of viewing the world, modes of analysis, and explanations. The North had to wrestle with the question of free labor, with some observers dodging and others confronting head-on the growing inequities in their emergent wage economy. But in the South, thinking about the slave economy was a very complicated affair because theirs was not simply a society with slavery but a slave society whose entire political, social, and moral economies were built to justify the presence of a permanent labor force based on race. Chattel slavery animated the entire lived experience of the South, as well as white Southerners' habits of mind to make sense of those experiences.

While Southerners had little use for the literature and social criticism of the Transcendentalists, they shared their affection for European Romanticism. But where Northerners employed European Romanticism to challenge the prevailing social order, Southerners read it as a confirmation that they needed to resist being pulled into Northern-style modernization and social change. Southerners, like their Northern counterparts, were cosmopolitan in their reading tastes, but with a sense of longing and elsewhereness much more intense, and much more prone to anxiety and foreboding. It was often hard for the mistress of the plantation household to delight in the subtle pleasures of Wordsworth's "Lines Composed a Few Miles

Above Tintern Abbey" (1798) when her home was a beehive of activity with slaves cooking in the kitchen, tending to crying children in the nursery, and loudly shuffling from room to room with baskets of laundry and cleaning supplies. Likewise, reading Coleridge's "The Rime of the Ancient Mariner" (1834) could make a Southern master happy to be landlocked on his cotton plantation while feeling similarly adrift and scared for his safety amid his dozens of slaves, who hated him more than they feared him. Southerners' wistful, if anxious, elsewhereness encouraged them to look to the historians of the distant past (Thucydides, Herodotus, Livy) and the recent past (David Hume, Edward Gibbon) to place their lives in Athens (Georgia) or Oxford (Mississippi) or Montpelier (Virginia) or Selma (Alabama, named for Celtic poet Ossian's *The Songs of Selma* [1760]) in the grander scheme of world history. If theirs was a cosmopolitan perspective, it was one in which certainty was tinged with doubt and a chronic yearning for rootedness was offset by persistent feelings of being trapped at the edges of civilization.

For the Virginia lawyer and slavery apologist George Fitzhugh, thinking in the South meant thinking about the Southern way of life and its superiority to that of the North. Rather than dodge the issue of slavery, he took it head-on. In *Sociology for the South* (1854), Fitzhugh thought that slavery was a more natural, organic way of organizing society than free labor, for it better preserved the mutual interdependence of one group with another. The master-slave relationship, much like feudal relationships in the past, recognized that the powerful group has both the ability and the responsibility to protect its subjects. He presented paternalist arguments for slavery as more humane than the "free" labor system emerging in the north: "[The slave economy] makes [our] society a band of brothers, working for the common good, instead of a bag of cats biting and worrying each other. The competitive system is a system of antagonism and war; ours of peace and fraternity. The first is the system of free society; the other that of slave society."[23] While Fitzhugh was no Marxist and Karl Marx no advocate of slavery in any form, Fitzhugh's challenges to the exploitation within capitalism echoed some of the criticisms Marx had advanced just six years earlier in *The Communist Manifesto* (1848).

Southern intellectual life and defenses of the "peculiar institution" went hand in glove, but never more so than in the writings of Louisa S. McCord. A highly educated South Carolinian mistress of a cotton plantation with more than two hundred slaves, McCord wrote ardent defenses of Southern slave society. In "Negro-Mania" (1852), one of her many essays on the necessity and moral superiority of slavery, she put it plainly:

> Is the negro made for slavery? God in heaven! What are we that, because we cannot understand the mystery of this Thy will, we should dare in rebellion and call it wrong, unjust, and cruel? The kindness of natures fits each creature to fulfill its destiny. The very virtues of the negro fit him for slavery, and his vices cry aloud for the checks of bondage.[24]

McCord systematically and passionately compared Southern and Northern culture and the different personalities they produced, such as her comparison of the Southern matron with Yankee "petticoated despisers of their sex—these would-be men. . . . Moral monsters they are." Had McCord known that female education was actually more widespread in the South than the North (because there were lower fears of Southern petticoated women entering public life), she would have had another barb with which to sting them. She sought to make it clear to her readers that slavery was in perfect harmony with nature and God's will, and that any threat to eradicating it would upset the Southerners' entire way of life, which was precisely as their Maker wanted it to be.[25]

The vast majority of slaves in America were legally forbidden to learn to read (and write), so it was nearly impossible for them to come in contact with elaborate intellectual justifications for their servitude and suffering like Fitzhugh's and McCord's. But by necessity they had to learn to "read" their masters', mistresses', and overseers' minds for sheer survival. Forced illiteracy did not mean that they had no elaborate mental and moral lives of their own. They did. Their mindscapes were created from the religious beliefs they brought with them from Africa, folk tales they told and remade in each telling to speak to the conditions of their enslavement, biblical songs or stories they learned from their owners, and their experience as human beings, albeit in the most inhumane of circumstances. Their greatest mental challenge lay not in constructing their own beliefs and viewpoints, but in jealously guarding them from their masters. As one African American folk song went:

> Got one mind for white folks to see,
> 'Nother for what I know is me;
> He don't know, he don't know my mind.
> When he see me laughing,
> Laughing just to keep from Crying.[26]

There was nothing more threatening to a master than to admit to owning a slave who thought for him- or herself. Slaves knew that even thinking for themselves could be a punishable offense, and yet they persisted. Thus, when trying to access the intellectual worlds of the antebellum South, there is not only a split screen between white masters and their black slaves but also a split screen within the slaves' minds, keeping their innermost thoughts to themselves and projecting whatever acceptable thoughts could keep them from further torment, or even death.

Even slave narratives composed by former slaves fortunate enough to have been taught to read and write, or ingenious enough to figure out how to do so on their own, had to perform their own doublespeak. They strove to be as forthcoming with their first-hand experiences of enslavement, while risking nothing that could jeopardize the millions still held in captivity to the Southern way of life. Olaudah Equiano's *The Interesting Narrative of the Life of*

Olaudah Equiano, or Gustavas Vassa, the African (1798), Frederick Douglass's *Narrative of the Life of Frederick Douglass, an American Slave* (1845), and Harriet Jacobs's *Incidents in the Life of a Slave Girl* (1861) are the three most prominent examples of the form. Authors toggled between religious assertions and political arguments, fierce logic and emotional petition, and ethnographic detail and broad generalizations, as they brought their readers as close to their pain as they could without making it pornographic.

Each of them, in their own way, expressed the very Romantic sensibilities and republican assumptions articulated by white authors. The main difference is that white authors had the luxury of coming to these ideas by way of books and polite conversation. The black authors of slave narratives, by contrast, had to come to them by way of a daily struggle for survival.

Though the gulfs between the worldviews of Southerns and Northerners and blacks and whites were deep and wide, all were, nevertheless, deeply entangled in a struggle for control over their destinies in America, as Americans.

Woman Thinking

It is often tempting to try to identify a thinker who can adequately represent the intellectual preoccupations and styles of thought particular to an era. However, such efforts never quite do justice to the variegated intellectual landscape in question, nor do they suffice to illuminate the mind of the thinker who is enlisted to be a representative. No single author can stand for an age. But if there was one figure who helps identify some of the central preoccupations of the republican Romanticism of antebellum America, it would be Margaret Fuller.

Even by splitting Fuller's résumé in half, and then splitting those halves in half, just one of those cropped and quartered segments of her intellectual record has the power to astonish us. How is it that one person managed to pack so many stunning intellectual accomplishments into her brief forty years? Fuller pioneered a dialogical mode of pedagogy called "conversations." She served as editor of the Transcendentalists' main organ, *The Dial*. She was widely recognized as a formidable interlocutor and the source of ideas for many of the major writers in the orbit of Boston and Concord. She was the one thinker Emerson knew personally whom he marveled at (perhaps with the exception of Thoreau), even if with a little discomfort at the imposing rigor and erudition of her mind. Fuller wrote the most important feminist manifesto of her day, *Woman in the Nineteenth Century* (1845), which has since become a classic of feminist philosophy. She served as a foreign correspondent in Europe, writing important dispatches about social and political developments there for readers back home. She was not content to be a witness to the democratic revolutions rocking Europe and the northern transatlantic world more broadly, so she participated in the Italian Risorgimento in Rome before dying as her ship returning from Italy hit stormy seas just off the coast of Fire Island, New York, in 1849. And those are just the highlights. Most remarkable of all is that she pulled off this intellectual productivity in a culture that thought she should be seen (though not too much in public) and not heard.

But what makes Fuller such a compelling thinker not only of her age but also for ours is that, without much Sturm und Drang, she harmonized the warring intellectual and moral imperatives that vexed so many other thinkers of her day. She was the very model of antebellum "self-culture": an average day for her involved studying French, Greek, and Italian; attending lectures on philosophy; practicing the piano and singing; taking long walks; conducting "conversations"; and writing in her journal. Ego-theism was never her motivation; rather, it was to perfect her self so that it could help perfect her society. Likewise, she cultivated a cosmopolitan orientation to establish as large a moral and intellectual frame of reference as possible to help her readers hear themselves thinking over the din of a clamoring materialism. Fuller regarded the labor of her words to be work as dignified and urgent as other forms of social protest; she drew no distinctions between thinking and doing, refusing to privilege one over the other in the making of a new nation. And though she similarly longed for a kind of Emersonian self-sovereignty, she could not do so from the perspective of his "transparent eyeball," nor did she seem to have any desire to do so. Balancing intellectual autonomy with the bounded perspective of dispossessed Native Americans, enslaved African Americans, and privileged white women who were nevertheless second-class citizens was good enough for her. Where Emerson called out to his reader to "Trust thyself: every heart vibrates to that iron string" and "Insist on yourself; never imitate," Fuller wondered quietly instead: "Where can I hide till I am given to myself?"[27] She thus had all of the Transcendentalist ambition to step outside the limitations of one's culture and circumstance, while understanding intimately the structural constraints making that possible for some and impossible for others.

Emerson dared in 1837 to imagine a time when America would produce its own Man Thinking. He scanned the horizons far and wide, eager for signs of his advent. In this regard, Emerson was both a visionary and a man of his day. By searching yonder, he failed to notice that right there next to him in the *Dial* office, editing one of his essays or debating with him a finer point of his argument, was his Man Thinking, in the shape of a woman.

Chapter 4

Contests of Intellectual Authority: 1850–90

In 1859, two historical events dramatically altered the course of American thought. The first took place on October 16 in Harpers Ferry (in today's West Virginia), when the abolitionist John Brown led a band of twenty-one men on a raid on a US arsenal, which he hoped would set the stage for a slave revolt. The second event took place in London, England, a little over a month later, with the publication of *On the Origin of Species by Means of Natural Selection, or the Preservation of Favoured Races in the Struggle for Life*. For Americans living at the time, the two events were yoked together. For many abolitionists, Charles Darwin's ideas proved that what Brown had martyred himself for was true: that black people were no more animals than whites, and that both shared a common origin and therefore deserved the same destiny as free people living in a free republic. For proslavery advocates, the two were connected as well, but in a very different way. They used Darwin's ideas to prove that even in a democracy, "survival of the fittest" was the law of the land, thus explaining why lesser races are inevitably subordinated to higher ones. Over the next decades, Americans would wrestle mightily with the implications of both Brown's actions and Darwin's words.

"The Civil War marks an era in the history of the American mind," wrote the novelist Henry James in 1879. "It introduced into the national consciousness a certain sense of proportion and relation, of the world being a more complicated place. . . . [The] American, in days to come, will be a more critical person than his complacent and confident grandfather. He has eaten of the tree of knowledge."[1] Henry James was one of America's most perspicacious writers, but on this score he was only partly correct. This may have been true for white Northerners and Southerners. It most certainly was true for a chastened Abraham Lincoln, who in 1863 at Gettysburg, Pennsylvania, lamented that the warring views of the North and South could not be reconciled with words rather than waged in blood on the battlefield.

But African Americans did not need a war to impress on them that the world was a "complicated place." In fact, the foremost African American intellectual of the nineteenth century, Frederick Douglass, had long tried to complicate whites' views of themselves and their America, and to show how inconsistent slavery was with those views. "What, to the American slave, is your Fourth of July?" Douglass, a former slave himself, asked a group of abolitionists in Rochester, New York, in 1852. Before they could shout back "freedom!" or "liberty!" he told them what Independence Day looked like from the slave's perspective: "a day that reveals to him, more than all other days in the year, the gross injustice and cruelty to which he is the constant victim. To him, your celebration is a sham; your boasted liberty an unholy license; your national greatness [a] swelling vanity. . . . [F]or revolting barbarity and shameless hypocrisy, America reigns without a rival."[2]

Abraham Lincoln dedicated his presidency to closing this gap between American ideals and reality, free and unfree labor, white rights and wronged blacks, all the while binding up the wounds between Northerners and Southerners. Born just a few hours apart from Charles Darwin on February 12, 1809, the Illinois lawyer turned national statesman knew of the British naturalist but never read his *Origins of Species* or was conversant in his theory on evolution. Though deeply committed to an enlightenment republican ideology tinged with the mystical Romanticism of his day, Lincoln nevertheless believed that American democracy, much like Darwin's natural world, was a process, an unfolding or, as he put it, an "undecided experiment."[3] In 1863, at the gravesite of the Union soldiers who had died in the Battle of Gettysburg, Lincoln maintained that the founders had bequeathed a "proposition that all men are created equal" and that it was the awesome task of his contemporaries on both sides of the Mason-Dixon line to "test" whether a "nation so conceived and so dedicated" could endure. The "unfinished work" of the dead Union soldiers left it to "the living" to ensure that the political foundations of America would have a democratic future and one that was capable of evolving out of its slaveholding origins.[4] Lincoln hoped until his final days that they could answer the proposition in the affirmative, all the while being haunted by the prospect that they would not.

One of the primary aims of intellectual history is to understand the ideas undergirding competing moral viewpoints, like those between abolitionists and proslavery advocates, and Darwin's American supporters and his detractors. It seeks to comprehend the factors that shape historical actors' intellectual options, and to see how their moral horizons and habits of thought played decisive roles both internally in their acts of intellectual volition and externally in their actions in the world. What factors inhibited intellectual agreement? What ideas or viewpoints were available to some but not others? What is the balance of power between need, desire, fear, folly, sagacity, and foresight in the making and unmaking of historical actors' intellectual worldviews? And how were their moral horizons constructed in the first place? The primary responsibility of the intellectual historian is not to issue verdicts on moral decision-making of the past but rather to comprehend how those actors came to their understanding of their world and their role in it. These contests of moral authority and the range of human responses to human problems are on full display in the "entangled bank" of late nineteenth-century American life.[5]

The Scientific Reception of Darwin's
Origin of Species

In 1835, a number of tiny finches living on a volcanic archipelago about five hundred miles west of Ecuador helped forever change the course of modern thought. They were not the only creatures to impress the twenty-two-year-old aspiring Anglican minister and unpaid naturalist Charles Darwin during his five-year journey with the British survey ship HMS *Beagle*. Indeed, they were much less visually captivating than the archipelago's five-hundred-pound tortoises lumbering around and the wacky and adorable blue-footed boobies doing their goofy mating dances. But Darwin noticed something quite remarkable about these otherwise unremarkable little songbirds. The sizes, beak shape, and claw formation of the finches living on the islands were somewhat different than those found on the mainland, as well as somewhat different from each other. Darwin concluded that these variations must be due to the particular food sources available on each of the islands. Pecking the juice out of cacti on one island surely required a particular beak shape different than the one needed for chewing tiny berries on another. The shape of the claw most advantageous for grasping seedlings was not the same as the best one for grabbing crawly insects. Darwin extrapolated from his findings that the finches must have evolved over time from a common mainland ancestor and developed in such a way as to favor those features that were best suited to survival on their particular island. Chance, he concluded, was involved in variations, nothing more. But the finches whose qualities gave them a competitive advantage in that terrain were more likely to survive and reproduce. Darwin settled on the name "natural selection" for this mechanism of evolution and generalized more broadly that all life on Earth likely started with a single origin and evolved from there. In 1859, he published his findings in *On the Origin of Species*.

Prior to Darwin, most educated people in America and Europe believed that God created the universe, with each species as it was when he first made the earth. Tortoises were tortoises. Elephants were elephants. Blue-footed boobies were blue-footed boobies. That is how God made them, and so that is how they had always been and were supposed to be. They assumed that humans too were made as the Creator meant them to be: in his own image from the time of Adam and Eve up until their own nineteenth-century age. Even the land on which they lived, the waters on which they sailed, and the sky and stars that provided them a sacred canopy were just as God created them; their universe was stable and immutable.

Darwin's theory of natural selection helped change all of that, but it took the efforts of his American popularizers, both detractors and advocates, to ensure that it would. Initially, two of the most important commentators on *Origin* were professors at Harvard University. Zoologist Louis Agassiz, Darwin's most formidable opponent, and biologist Asa Gray, his most dogged defender, helped make the university a hub of Darwinian contestation in the early years of its American reception. Like the vast majority of scientists in nineteenth-century America, Agassiz and Gray were Christians who believed that science was but another way to access God's universe. They simply had very different views about how Darwin's theories could be made to harmonize with their understanding of the natural world and their religious commitments.

Agassiz was known for his breakthrough studies of the fossil record of fish, his glacial theory, and his encyclopedic classification of the animal kingdom. He commanded respect among scientists and enjoyed an enormous popular appeal. He took it upon himself to assure unsettled Americans that *Origin* was nothing more than a compendium of "marvelous bear, cuckoo, and other stories."[6] With a predominantly idealist and theological approach to biology, he stood fast to his long-held scientific position that every species represented an idea produced by God's "premeditation, power, wisdom, greatness, prescience, omniscience, providence." On top of that, every living thing had its place in a rank order descending from the highest to the lowest, each with its own "natural connection" to the "One God, whom man may know, adore, and love."[7] He agreed with Darwin that species changed over time, but not that chance had anything to do with these changes. Rather, he posited that after every geological period, God rethought his designs and made whatever changes, if any, he deemed appropriate. When God rolled out the newer model, it may have had a resemblance to the prior one, but only because both were his creations. Whatever connection they had, then, was to their Maker, not to each other as a result of evolution.

Agassiz's colleague Gray found Darwin's natural selection more persuasive than Agassiz's "mind of God" classifications, and he preferred it to earlier evolutionists' theories that change resulted from the innate workings of the species themselves and not from their interactions with their environments. As early as 1860, Gray published a review of *Origin* in the *American Journal of Science and Arts*, establishing him as Darwin's foremost American ambassador and helping to provide scientific respectability to the British naturalist's radical ideas. Gray, unlike Darwin, remained an orthodox Protestant and therefore worked hard to demonstrate that Darwin's natural selection could be compatible with religious belief. Though Darwin was grateful for Gray's advocacy, it made him uneasy because he thought that Gray simply had no empirical evidence for his claims that evolution was a divinely driven process. Gray also broke with Darwin on the origin of humans, pressing for a "special origination" thesis, which meant that the rules of natural selection did not apply to them. But despite some of his own disagreements with Darwin's model and Darwin's ambivalence about Gray's rejiggering of his ideas to make them line up with his religion so that they were more palatable to broader audiences, Gray proved instrumental in encouraging American scientists to invest further scientific investigation into these questions. So too did

Agassiz, as his own students at Harvard eventually came to accept the Darwinian framework and conducted their scientific inquiries accordingly. By 1877, a leading paleontologist would announce that "to doubt evolution to-day is to doubt science."[8] Few professional American scientists from that point on would make claims for the special creation of species.

Of Faith and Finches

In the popular retelling of Darwinism, *Origin* was like a powder keg that exploded readers' religious certainties the moment they lifted its front cover. Nothing could be further from the truth. Lay Christian readers had no reason to concern themselves with Darwinian evolution until their religious leaders told them they needed to, and initially, for most American clergymen and theologians, natural selection was just another theory from just another fallen man just trying to make sense of his fallen world. True, this particular fallen man had described nature as an "entangled bank" of creatures engaged in a "Struggle for Life" with no higher purpose or order governing the "war of nature."[9] But Darwin had affirmed that this struggle is what produces the beauty and harmony of the natural world. Nevertheless, given the yawning abyss between this characterization and the one found in the Bible, many had no trouble swatting it away. This was the case with the Presbyterian theologian at the Princeton seminary, Charles Hodge, who titled his 1874 book *What Is Darwinism?*. For him, the answer was patently clear: "It is Atheism."[10]

For much of the 1860s, 1870s, and even 1880s, liberal theologians had a relatively easy time of it, finding all sorts of ways to refashion Darwin's ideas as an apologia for their faith, much as Gray had already started to do in 1860. Once a growing number of scientists followed Gray over Agassiz, liberal Protestants found ways to unlock the hidden divine plan within Darwin's evolutionary scheme.

John Fiske, an American historian and popularizer of Darwinism, titled his 1886 study *The Idea of God as Affected by Modern Knowledge* and his 1899 work *Through Nature to God* in an effort to show that modern science could improve rather than undermine faith. In a variety of ways, Fiske used familiar religious language to explain Darwinism: "The principle of natural selection is in one respect intensely Calvinistic; it elects the one and damns the ninety and nine."[11] Henry Ward Beecher, the New York Congregational minister and popular lecturer (and brother of antislavery author Harriet Beecher Stowe), exemplified the growing tendency of liberal theologians to embrace evolution as an endorsement of their faith. Like other liberal theologians of the era, Beecher had long been at work dismissing the forbidding God of unreconstructed Calvinism and welcoming a more nurturing, tender, helpmate, and his version of Darwinism fit nicely in that project. Beecher was neither a penetrating thinker nor a careful reader of Darwin, but this helped him as he drafted his popular *Evolution and Religion* (1885), which reassured his largely white, middle-class readers that evolution simply proved their dearly held view of moral progress (despite the fact that Darwin thought it directionless and without any higher purpose). Beecher's liberal Christian Darwinism assured his late nineteenth-century audiences that fellowship and compassion, not greed and ruthlessness, were the human traits most necessary for racial progress and survival.

As the cases of Hodge, Fiske, and Beecher demonstrate, religious faith is more than a belief—it is an entire cosmology. When that faith is strong, as it was with the vast majority of mid-nineteenth-century American scientists, clergy, and laypeople, then all new ideas, both radical and seemingly inconsequential, are read through the prism of that worldview. Looking at the past through the lens of intellectual history demonstrates time and time again that the human imagination is extraordinarily deft at making new ideas jibe with prior intellectual and moral commitments, and when the two cannot or simply will not be reconciled, it is almost always the prior worldview that wins out. Henry James's brother, the brilliant psychologist and philosopher William James, understood this without fail: "in this matter of belief we are all extreme conservatives." The acceptance of a new idea almost always "preserves the older stock of truths with a minimum of modification, stretching them just enough to make them admit the novelty, but conceiving that in ways as familiar as the case leaves possible. An *outrée* explanation, violating all our preconceptions, would never pass for a true account of a novelty."[12]

There are rare cases, though, when an individual has only a tenuous hold on an inherited worldview but has not yet settled into a new one to replace it that there is a chance—sometimes nothing more than a lightning-flash moment—that space cracks open for something truly *outrée* to gain footing in her or his psyche. This is the exceptional case when the knowing mind admits that it does not know, and feels a moral obligation to hold true to that condition of uncertainty. And this is precisely what happened with Civil War veteran, lawyer, and popular orator Robert Ingersoll. The son of a Presbyterian minister, Ingersoll drifted from his father's faith as he witnessed how religion pandered to prejudice and justified injustices like slavery. In one of his most noteworthy speeches, "The Gods" (1872), Ingersoll told his audience something that the Civil War made hard to deny:

> Each nation has created a god, and the god has always resembled his creators. He hated and loved what they hated and loved, and he was invariably found on the side of those in power. Each god was intensely patriotic, and detested all nations but his own. All these gods demanded praise, flattery, and worship. Most of them were pleased with sacrifice, and the smell of innocent blood has ever been considered a divine perfume.[13]

The way clergy often handled new scientific discoveries that suggested that the Bible was a most unreliable account of the natural world also appalled Ingersoll: "Anything they could not dodge, they swallowed, and anything they could not swallow, they dodged."

When he added all of the mischief and misery religious faith had unleashed on the world, Ingersoll maintained that he had no choice but to become a professing "agnostic."[14]

Referred to as the "Great Agnostic" by his admirers and "Robert Injuresoul" by his clerical detractors, Ingersoll's stance—though prominent—was a rare exception at the time. For the remainder of the century, his agnosticism became more of an intellectual force rather than a new faith. It was one that proved very productive for other liberal intellectuals as they, like Ingersoll and socially progressive Protestants, fought against racism and the death penalty, and for women's rights. In time, Ingersoll's view that Darwinism demanded a more rigorous accounting of both the natural world and the moral worlds of the human descendants of apes living in it helped pave the way for change. It enabled a variety of late nineteenth- and early twentieth-century freethinkers and secular humanists fight to keep the public sphere genuinely public, and not simply an extension of the church's dominion.

Varieties of Evolutionary Social Thought

Although Darwinism made inroads into religious and scientific thought, it had a much more immediate and transformative effect in the realm of social ideas. It helped scholars in the emerging disciplines of sociology, anthropology, political economy, and psychology move with greater force and clarity in the direction they were already heading. Darwin helped them as they brought their understanding of social processes in line with the dramatic changes in American life due to industrial capitalism, urbanization, and mass immigration. For some that meant taking an un-Romantic, unafraid view of social development as merely another expression of the law of the jungle. For others, it meant the exact opposite, taking the position that efforts to overcome the struggle and strife of modernization or to reduce their damage were the mark of a truly evolved society. But there were two things both could agree on. First, they concurred, that change—not stasis—was the prime motor of the natural world, and thus working with it, rather than trying to prevent it, was the surest route to human progress. And second, they agreed that verisimilitude, not idealism, must be the prime motor of their post-Darwinian intellectual projects.

Yale University professor of political economy William Graham Sumner emerged in 1872 as the strongest voice in this period of what became known as Social Darwinism (though the ideas had only a tenuous connection to Darwin and tracked more closely to Herbert Spencer, the British sociologist, who coined the phrase "survival of the fittest"). Sumner had trained in theology and biblical criticism in Germany and England before doing a brief stint as an Episcopalian priest. But as he found the growing scientific positivism of the age more intellectually compelling than religion, he left the clergy to pursue the social sciences at Yale, where he became a hugely popular and influential professor. Sumner helped establish the budding field of sociology by proposing that the rules that govern the natural world also rule society, and that the evolution of humans is no different than the evolution of lower animals—both progress through conflict and contest. As a result, he argued that the study of human affairs, just like the study of organic compounds and orangutans, must be a scientific enterprise.

Sumner's science of society mixed Protestant ethics, classical economics, and democratic individualism in its advocacy of an unflinching "Darwinian" framework. In his 1883 treatise *What Social Classes Owe to Each Other*, his answer was unapologetic: absolutely nothing. His chapter titles were about as forthcoming as they could possibly be in announcing his endorsement of laissez-faire: "That Poverty Is the Best Policy," "That It Is Not Wicked to Be Rich," and "He Who Would Be Well Taken Care of Must Take Care of Himself." In *The Absurd Effort to Make the World Over* (1894), Sumner pressed forward with his laissez-faire positions

Evolutionary thought influenced late nineteenth-century American artists in different ways. Albert Bierstadt's valedictory painting, *The Last of the Buffalo* (1888, above), shows the era's increasing preoccupation with evolution and extinction. Whereas Bierstadt's work is executed in an earlier style of Hudson River School high Romanticism, Thomas Eakins's *The Gross Clinic* (1875, right), by contrast, reflects the growing commitment to brute realism and unadorned verisimilitude, by depicting a prosaic (and unelegaic) scene of a surgery at Jefferson Medical College. *Corcoran Collection, National Gallery of Art; Philadelphia Museum of Art*

as he tried to persuade Gilded Age social reformers that their desire to legislate social policies and economic structures to keep Americans from tumbling into poverty, illness, and destitution was touching, but pointless. He wrote:

> The first instinct of the modern man is to get a law passed to forbid or prevent what, in his wisdom, he disapproves. A thing which is inevitable, however, is one which we cannot control. We have to make up our minds to it, adjust ourselves to it, and sit down to live with it. Its inevitableness may be disputed, in which case we must re-examine it; but if our analysis is correct, when we reach what is inevitable we reach the end, and our regulations must apply to ourselves, not to the social facts.[15]

Sumner even outpaced Spencer's worship of the "actual," "inevitable," and "reality" by hoisting "facts" over theory with greater zeal than the inventor of Social Darwinism himself. But together Sumner and Spencer engaged in a transatlantic campaign to persuade moderns that "the law of the survival of the fittest was not made by man," and so the only thing man can do is interfere with it, and thereby "produce the survival of the unfittest."[16]

Evolutionary theories similarly influenced the course of linguistics, ethnology, and archeology as they came together into a new modern social science: anthropology. They helped discredit polygenesis theories, but not necessarily the social inequalities and racist attitudes they hoped to defend.

The arrival of Darwin's ideas managed to undermine the antebellum American version of the "science of man." The most prominent example of this midcentury doctrine can be found in the scientific racism of the physician Josiah Nott and his collaborator, Egyptologist George Gliddon. In a curious departure from the biblical authority of the Christianity they aimed to safeguard, Nott and Gliddon, like Agassiz before them, asserted that there were separate creations for the different races, with Europeans the most superior physically and mentally. African Americans started out as an inferior race and thus they would forever remain inferior, and Native Americans were so compromised as to be doomed to extinction. "Polygenesis" was the name for this imaginary schema, but it proved to be no match for Darwin's evidence of the shared origin of all humanity. But while Darwinism managed to upend polygenesis in America, scientists still persuaded of the superiority of whites and the inferiority of all other racial groups managed to rework evolutionary claims to justify their positions.

Nevertheless, Social Darwinism did not produce uniform ideas about policies toward other races and ethnicities. For example, many experts on Native Americans employed evolutionary ideas with the humanitarian goal of "helping" Indians through assimilationist policies, while others used evolution to justify establishing a system of reservations to protect them from the encroachments of Euro-Americans. Similarly, advocates of American imperial ventures abroad were confident that Anglo Saxons would be better stewards of foreign lands while helping to civilize their native populations. And

Darwin's *On the Origin of Species* (1859) challenged polygenesis, a theory of racial difference delineated in this tableau classifying human races and fauna according to their regional "realms." Louis Agassiz, the foremost polygenesis theorist in America, believed that "what are called human races, down to their specializations as nations, are distinct primordial forms of the type of man." *Josiah Clark Nott and George Robert Gliddon,* Types of mankind, Or, Ethnological researches, based upon the ancient monuments, paintings, sculptures, and crania of races, and upon their natural, geographical, philological and Biblical history (Philadelphia and London, 1854). *University of Wisconsin–Madison, Special Collections*

yet the greatest American champion of Social Darwinism—William Graham Sumner himself—was a passionate anti-imperialist, as he believed that imperialism fostered an evolutionary regression toward primitive militarism and authoritarianism.

Darwinist ideas were also employed to advance some of the most sophisticated economic theories, and indeed some of the wittiest, most clever (if mercilessly scathing) cultural critiques of the era: the writings of the sociologist and economist Thorstein Veblen. Having trained under Sumner at Yale, Veblen produced lines one would expect from his mentor, such as "The life of man in society, just like the life of other species, is a struggle for existence, and therefore it is a process of selective adaptation."[17] But that is where the similarities end.

Veblen pushed for an even more rigorous and nuanced application of evolutionary theory, dispensing with the tendency to use it to either justify or criticize economic competition. Instead, he employed it to remake modern economists' "habits of thought." For Veblen the value of evolutionary theory was that it challenged not the ideas from classical political economy but rather its methods of inquiry. Veblen thus focused on how human beings, as well as their economic institutions and social practices, tracked with the vicissitudes of modern life. His *Theory of the Leisure Class* (1899) revealed the fruits of this new way of thinking by examining the economic and cultural implications of the propertied classes' "wastefulness" and "conspicuous consumption" on the well-being of society as a whole. He used evolutionary theory to claim that in the "savage" stage of civilization, every member of the tribe had to work to ensure the survival of the race. But with the coming of the "barbarian" stage (the stage late nineteenth-century America was in), a surplus of resources and labor enabled what he called the "leisure class" to exempt themselves from work and to live off the fruits of others. Rather than assume that the uneven distribution of wealth indicated an uneven distribution of human talent and ingenuity, Veblen argued that it reflected an evolutionary maladaptation of a "retarding influence" upon social betterment.[18] And for Veblen, nothing was so retarding as the culture of Victorianism that he took as his enemy.

Victorian Culture and Its Critics

Queen Victoria of England did not reign over the United States, but the worldview she and many of her British subjects sought to embody significantly influenced American thought and culture from the mid- to late nineteenth century. While both elite and bourgeois Americans were drawn to Victorian notions of order, uplift, and refinement, it was middle-class boosters who made it such a potent cultural force. As industrial capitalism took command, it fueled dramatic technological advancement, geographic expansion, and the creep of markets and commodification into all facets of life. It also brought with it intensified class stratification in America between an upper class on the one end and the laboring classes and the poor at the other, with a middle class in between gaining a distinct group identity and sense of mission. Members of the new middle class looked to what they regarded as the excesses and entitlements of the rich and the decrepitude and rudeness of the poor, deeming both a threat to the well-being of a democratic, civil society. They thus championed a new didactic, prescriptive, Victorian ideal of "culture" as a means of moral improvement and a safeguard of democratic virtue, with themselves as its ideal custodians. In *Culture and Anarchy* (1869), the British author Matthew Arnold provided them with a vision of culture as "*a study of perfection*," the repository of "the best that has been thought and known," and thus with a means to counteract the deleterious effects of modernization.[19]

The emergent ideal of culture found its most potent expression in the institutions designed to cultivate and disseminate it. Victorian Americans founded an extraordinary network of newly established universities and colleges, museums, symphonies, theaters, literary societies, and parks during this period, all with the purpose of channeling the competitive and materialist energies of a modernizing America into leisure pursuits that cultivated minds, nurtured bodies, and nourished souls. One of the quintessential Victorian institutions that combined instruction and refinement was the Chautauqua Institution in western New York, founded in 1874 by Methodist minister John Heyl Vincent. What began as an ecumenical institute to train Sunday school teachers turned into an extensive system of "outdoor university" programs throughout the Midwest (and eventually the country), bringing in some of the most eminent intellectual and cultural figures of the period to lecture to large crowds in a festive—even celebratory—environment. Uplift, enlightenment, and moral improvement were the catchwords of Chautauqua.

The same could be said of Frederick Law Olmsted's landscape designs. The foremost landscape architect of the era, Olmsted designed scenic parks (most notably Central Park in New York City and Golden State Park in San Francisco), stately university campuses, and bucolic grounds for state capitols, hospitals, and libraries, all in an effort to provide little pastoral retreats from the demands and dangers of city life. He drew from Jeremy Bentham's theories of control and reform as he imagined that his green spaces could serve a pedagogical and even disciplinary function. Olmsted set out clearly marked paths, neatly manicured lawns, decorative trees planted as objects of beauty and canopies to provide protection from the elements, and marble fountains to offer the soothing sights and sounds of water tumbling down its tiers—all staged to offer open spaces for democratic conviviality, while providing cues for order to train urban dwellers in refinement. Both Vincent's Chautauquas and Olmsted's landscapes aspired to make Victorian "recreation" not simply a Gilded Age pastime but also a way to literally re-create the self in terms harmonious with ideals and images of perfection.

Though the work of culture took place in public venues, Victorians thought it should also be instilled in private homes. The cultural logic of gentility was on full display in the Victorian domestic sphere. The home was to be a sanctuary from the heartless world of capitalist competition. Whereas the middle-class husband and father had to make his way in the public world of aggressiveness and acquisitiveness in the emerging marketplace, the role of the wife and mother was to provide a redemptive sphere of pleasing beauty, sentimental comforts, and moral sustenance as a retreat from such ugliness. If the Victorian man must pursue the base needs for the family's material prosperity, the Victorian woman must seek the higher ideals for the family's moral progression. The liberal Protestant minister and theologian Horace Bushnell explained the Victorians' logic: men represented the "force principle" and women the "beauty principle."[20]

Material culture and social conventions are sometimes the best register of intellectual commitments of a period, and this is very much the case with the Victorian parlor. The domestic parlor was the Victorians' sanctuary of sentimental grace and tenderness, as well as a private stage for members of the family to perform their roles. Everything was scripted. At some prominent focal point in the room sat the oversized, decorative family Bible, which was too heavy and cumbersome to actually read, but looked positively lovely as a display piece. Every furnishing in the room had a specific function: decorative armchairs for men, delicate settees for the ladies, miniature upholstered seating for the children, windowseats for the family cat to curl up on, and reception chairs at the entrance for visitors. It was not enough to have walls, ceilings, and windows: carved or fluted molding, heavy baseboards, and ornamented door and window frames to adorn them were a must. Add to that the cavalry of curtains, pillows, carpets, and table runners to ensure protection for all the room's surfaces and soft comfort for its human inhabitants. In an ideal scenario, large paintings would cover the walls, as in the new museums, and leather-bound books accented by the occasional miniature Greek sculpture reproduction would line the shelves, as in the new urban libraries and reading rooms. In this sacred space, everyone knew their social cues: things one could say and not say, a volume in which to say it, and a bodily comportment for carrying on conversations, and all of this differed depending on one's gender and age. The elaborate vocabulary of furnishings and practices had more important work to do than to be merely outwardly pleasing. It had to stand as the register of the family's—and especially the wife's and mother's—inner cultivation.

Staging all of these paraphernalia and practices could be hard labor for Victorian wives and mothers. But making terrible fun of it was an equally demanding job for the growing chorus of critics who found this whole spectacle of Victorian uplift intellectually obscene and morally indefensible. In 1873, Mark Twain satirized the manners and morals of the whole period in his novel *The Gilded Age*.

A year later, E. L. Godkin, founder and editor of *The Nation*, surveyed an American landscape increasingly populated by popular lyceum lectures, newspapers and periodicals with "a kind of smattering of all sorts of knowledge," large art museums in the cities, and the miniature art museums of families' private parlors and cited them all as evidence of America's pretentious and vacuous "Chromo-Civilization." According to Godkin, this "pseudo-culture" created a "society of ignoramuses" who substituted the accumulation of facts for the assimilation of real knowledge, and the consumption of goods for the cultivation of character.[21]

Another exasperated critic of Victorianism, especially the habits of mind it cultivated, was the Spanish-born philosopher George Santayana. Together with William James and Josiah Royce, Santayana taught philosophy at Harvard University before he gave up his professorship and moved to Europe to become a full-time writer in 1912. But before he left, he gave his adopted homeland a parting gift in the form of a withering critique of its thought and culture: "The Genteel Tradition in American Philosophy" (1911). Santayana reproached the mental habits of Victorian Americans who viewed culture as a corrective to, rather than as a condition of, daily life. In his view, this "genteel" Victorianism grew out of two sources, and neither of them was good.

The first was a despiritualized Calvinism, which retained its lust for order and severe moralizing, but no longer the "agonized conscience" and "sense of sin" that gave earlier Protestantism its form. The second and more dominant source, however, was Emersonian Transcendentalism, which, in his view, endorsed a subjective view of knowledge and an aggrandized conception of self. Santayana believed that the restless, revolutionary American temperament proved to be the ideal host environment for early nineteenth-century Romanticism, which "felt that Will was deeper than Intellect; it focused everything here and now, and asked all things to show their credentials at the bar of the young self. . . These things are truly American."[22] In Santayana's genealogy, these two intellectual legacies crossed paths and consolidated their capital in the form of the genteel tradition: a moralistic and evasive intellectual temperament, suffused with light yet casting no shadows, an unthreatened if unthreatening view of the universe and man's place within it. Santayana's main complaint with the genteel tradition was not only that it made an easy peace with the universe but also that it had too reverential an attitude to the culture and ideas of Europe, which neither grew out of nor had any bearing on American material realities. According to Santayana, in a post-Darwinian age of advanced capitalism, it simply made no sense to treat intellectual pursuits as custodianship rather than the creation of ideas and culture.

Henry David Thoreau greatly admired John Brown and Charles Darwin. Just two weeks after Brown's siege on Harpers Ferry, Thoreau gave a speech, "A Plea for Captain John Brown," in which he made clear why Brown was the very best example of a Transcendentalist. Brown was "a transcendentalist above all, a man of ideas and principles,—that was what distinguished him. Not yielding to a whim or transient impulse, but carrying out the purpose of a life."[23] Thoreau had no problem recognizing, with Brown, that this "purpose" was individual freedom in harmony with a higher power. But his steadfast belief in human purpose did not prevent him from cherishing Darwin's theories, which presented a world with no telos but instead one marked by chance, accident, and randomness. Thoreau was entranced with Darwin's eye for details in nature, for his experimentation, and for characterizing the natural world in terms resonant with his own understanding of life: as something unsettled and ever becoming. Indeed, the American Transcendentalist was so taken with the British naturalist's attention to the tiniest drop of dew and croak of a baby frog that it inspired him to return to his own recordings of nature in his journals and compare them to Darwin's.

Thoreau died of the flu exacerbated by his tuberculosis in 1862, living long enough neither to learn the outcome of the Civil War nor to feel any pressure to square his feelings for Brown's higher purpose with Darwin's purposeless (though in his view sublime) universe. That task would fall to sensitive Americans in the following decades, who sought to use evolutionary theory as a way to foster a more just democracy.

Chapter 5

Modernist Revolts: 1890–1920

John Brown's raid on Harpers Ferry on October 16, 1859, and the publication of Darwin's *On the Origin of Species* a little over a month later, set off a chain of events that would forever transform American intellectual life. That same year, John Dewey, the pragmatist philosopher and progressive reformer, was born in Burlington, Vermont. It was a perfectly unremarkable event at the time—the birth of a baby boy—but this one would grow up to have a rather remarkable career as a philosopher, educational reformer, and social advocate. Dewey's labors, like Brown's and Darwin's before him, would greatly influence many Americans' notions of free will and determinism, truth and falsehood, and the possibility for a shared morality in a pluralistic universe. Having come of age in the intellectual world that the Civil War and Darwinian ideas forged, Dewey constructed a philosophy that would similarly challenge old ethical certainties, while emphasizing the individual's ability to effect positive change in an inscrutable cosmos.

Dewey and his contemporaries worked within and against the dramatic fin-de-siècle realignments of American intellectual life. It was then that the possibilities, as well as terrors, of the "blooming, buzzing confusion" of modernity came into fuller view, and with them, what Dewey would call a radically "new intellectual temper," which he himself exemplified.[1]

Not only were intellectual tempers and the ideas they wrestled with changing dramatically during this period, but so too were thinkers' conceptions of themselves and their social functions.

Up until this time, "intellectual" was part of the stock words of American English, but only as an adjective to describe a type of intelligence, mental style, and erudition. But during the heated controversy of the Dreyfus Affair in France, Émile Zola and his fellow "Dreyfusards" produced their *Manifest des intellectuels* in 1898, and with it, a new sociological term to consider the thinker's relationship to a broader public. No matter that Charles Maurras threw back "*intellectuels*" in his *Action française* as a term of snickering derision. For a new generation of emerging writers and thinkers in America, witnessing the whole messy affair had one benefit: it gave them a crucial term of self-definition for their roles in modern society.

For many younger thinkers and writers, the academy and the established presses were too implicated in a business culture driven by profit, and so they adopted the term *intellectual* as an oppositional, anti-institutional badge of honor. They looked to Europe to reveal clues about this new social type, and her or his relationship to the broader culture. There was no shortage of examples: Karl Marx, Friedrich Nietzsche, Oscar Wilde, and even Zola himself. To be sure, Marx was forced to flee Germany and later France, Nietzsche ended up clinically insane, Wilde was imprisoned, and Zola had to flee to England to avoid a prison sentence and heavy fines. But this only heightened the allure of the oppositional intellectual and provided them with a romantic image of themselves as the conscience of American culture.

Both affiliated and freelance intellectuals shared a number of concerns, however, which they recognized were particular to the role of the professional thinker in the United States. What are the duties and limitations of a democratic intellectual? If class and caste do not confer status, then what are the sources of authority for the intellectual in a democracy? How could the worlds of higher education and mass opinion be bridged without compromising the former and alienating the latter? The term *intellectual* invested them with a sense of responsibility to help their fellow Americans accept a modernizing world of social change and dissonance while finding new grounds to negotiate their differences and extending that spirit of democratic negotiation to the wider world.

The World's Columbian Exposition: A Festival of Ideas

The 1893 World's Columbian Exposition held in Chicago commemorated the four hundredth anniversary of Columbus's arrival in the New World. Its organizers wanted to pay tribute to America's imperialistic origins while also announcing its own grand entrance onto the world stage as a global economic power. The fair showcased sixty-five thousand international artifacts and inventions while also celebrating American technological prowess. Visitors could marvel over a "moveable sidewalk"; a dishwashing machine; all the ingredients for pancakes in one box and a friendly new character, "Aunt Jemima," to advertise them; and the world's first Ferris wheel, a behemoth of iron and steel, to rival the Eiffel Tower built for the Paris Exposition of 1889. The noted Chicago architect Daniel Burnham served as the fair's project director and hired Fredrick Law Olmsted to work his magic as the fair's landscape designer. With its "White City" of gleaming neoclassical buildings, "marble" facades and columns (made of white paint over plaster of Paris, glue, and hemp), decorative fountains and sculptures, and carefully groomed and maintained grounds, the fair celebrated, above all, Victorian values of order and refinement. The animating belief of the fair's organizers and visitors was that material progress and moral progress went hand in hand.

The fair was a celebration of technological wonders and commercial delights, but it was also a festival of ideas, displaying the intellectual commitments and preoccupations of the period. Some of the exhibits were more retrospective than prospective, such as the ethnographic displays built on the evolutionary logic of Victorian-era anthropology, then a budding field of the social sciences. Visitors could walk along the Midway Plaisance and see how different ethnic, racial, and national groups (in the form of live human displays) were organized from the most "primitive" to the most "advanced," thus providing a scientific apology for civilizing, imperial missions abroad and virulent ethnocentrism and racism at home.

But a number of the events showed a self-consciously "progressive" side of American thought, providing a window onto new intellectual worlds emerging at the time. The World's Parliament of Religions, a congress held at the fair, became the subject of great fascination and curiosity in the press. It demonstrated the emergence of a cosmopolitan sensibility and an appreciation of religious diversity by introducing fair visitors to the different worldviews and spiritual practices of people from all corners of the globe. Speakers included Buddhist monks from Japan and Sri Lanka, a Zoroastrian priest from India, an archbishop from the Greek Orthodox Church, a "Yankee Mohammadan" (i.e., an American convert to Islam), a bishop of the African Methodist Episcopal Church, a rabbi, and more. Papers on "The Essential Oneness of Ethical Ideas among All Men," "Points of Contact between Christianity and Mohammedanism," and "Religious Duty to the Negro" reflected the shared desire among participants to find universals among all religions, and to ensure that those religious universals were brought to bear on a modernizing world. As one Unitarian contributor put it: "One is born a Pagan, another a Jew, a third a Mussulman. The true philosopher sees in each a fellow-seeker after God."[2]

The organizers hoped that the Parliament of Religions would be more than a "one and done" gesture of religious ecumenism and solidarity, and they got what they wanted in the form of establishing interfaith relationships that would flower in years to come. It was at the conference that a twenty-seven-year-old student by the name of D. T. Suzuki, who accompanied his Zen Buddhist mentor as an interpreter and secretary, first met Paul Carus, a German American

One of the most highly anticipated events of the World's Columbian Exposition in Chicago, the World's Parliament of Religions of September 1893 provided a forum for international religious leaders to share their faith traditions with other clergy and fairgoers. With more than forty religious traditions represented and a daily attendance of several thousand participants, the parliament helped formally inaugurate modern interfaith dialogue in the United States. *Presbyterian Historical Society, Presbyterian Church, Philadelphia*

philosopher and publisher, who would be instrumental in exposing Suzuki to Western philosophy and the American religious landscape. A few years after the Parliament, Suzuki moved to Carus's residence in LaSalle, Illinois, for what turned out to be an eleven-year stay, where he worked as a translator and household help. Carus introduced him to William James, whose *Varieties of Religious Experience* (1902) helped Suzuki formulate his claim years later that experience—not scripture, theology, or ritual—was the cardinal feature of Buddhism. And he exposed Suzuki to the very religious pluralism in America that James had written about. Suzuki returned to Japan for the next three decades but came back to the United States midcentury, where he showed the value of those eleven years of learning the landscape of American culture. Suzuki returned as the most prominent ambassador of Zen Buddhism in the West, influencing figures as diverse as Martin Heidegger, Carl Gustav Jung, Alan Watts, Karen Horney, Erich Fromm, and the Beat poets, among so many others.

The Chicago Columbian Exposition also provided a platform for the latest in modern historical research. At a meeting of the American Historical Association held in conjunction with the fair, Frederick Jackson Turner, a thirty-one-year-old history professor from the University of Wisconsin, delivered his seminal lecture, *The Significance of the Frontier in American History* (1893), which would transform historical scholarship, as well as ideas about American culture and character. Turner wrote this piece in response to the 1890 federal census, which reported that there was no more Western land to be settled and so the frontier had closed. For Turner, this demanded a reckoning with the meaning of the frontier for American history.

Turner asserted that life along the frontier created antipathy toward any organizing efforts or assertions of power by an external, centralized authority. The result is that to the frontier the American intellect owes its striking characteristics. That . . . practical, inventive turn of mind, quick to find expedients; that masterful grasp of material things, . . . ; that restless, nervous energy; that dominant individualism, working for good and for evil, and withal that buoyancy and exuberance which comes with freedom—these are traits of the frontier, or traits called out elsewhere because of the existence of the frontier.[3] This restless, individualistic impulse set the terms for the nascent forms of modern democracy in the United States and shaped a particular mindset and personality among the people.

Though often remembered as a piece of triumphalist Americana, Turner's frontier thesis reflected his deep ambivalence about the fate of democracy with the closing of the frontier, and the fate of an America that prized practical knowledge over speculative and introspective thought. And though often considered a document about American democracy, it was also very much a meditation on the American mind. For Turner, the sheer abundance of land helped create an American way of thinking that was fundamentally individualistic, restless, practical, and impious toward traditions of the past.

There is much to suggest that these intellectual habits were good for survival on the frontier in the nineteenth century, but little to reassure his audience at the World's Fair that these were auspicious ways of thinking for progressive nation-building at the dawn of the twentieth century.

Pragmatism: A New Theory of Knowledge and a New Idea of "Truth"

Had Turner been speaking in the new language of turn-of-the-century American philosophy rather than history, he might have used another word to describe the intellectual processes and temperament he was after: *pragmatism*. Alongside Transcendentalism, pragmatism became the most important and influential philosophical tradition ever produced in America. Indeed, pragmatism can be seen as the philosophical heir of the Transcendentalists' antiestablishment impulse, with its recognition of the artificiality and potential tyranny of intellectual conventions. But pragmatism took this logic two steps further by developing both a more rigorous epistemology and methodology. It focused on the products of mental activity, as well as on the processes by which they are created. Pragmatism abandoned the search for universal, timeless truth and emphasized instead that a proposition is true if the practical consequences it implies or predicts do in fact follow in experience. A philosophy that welcomed the dynamism of truth, pragmatism reflects the vibrant, contested, and democratic society from which it came, while seeking to advance the better angels of its nature.

It is never easy to pinpoint with certainty all of the intellectual factors in play when a dramatically new way of viewing the world comes into existence. But in the case of pragmatism, Darwin's account of evolution, and the revolution it wrought in all areas of late nineteenth-century thought, played a crucial role. Darwin had offered a vision of the natural world as ever-changing and argued that randomness and chance, but also utility, are the forces that make for its dynamism. He did not just theorize his view of evolution; he also provided evidence to support his claims. This impulse to lay bare the dynamic workings of the world by use of scientific testing and evidence would go by many names in the late nineteenth-century world: scientism, naturalism, scientific naturalism, positivism, and, of course, Darwinism. But central to all of them was that in an unstable natural world, the range of inquiry must be limited to focus on truth claims that can be empirically verifiable.

John Dewey best summed this up in "The Influence of Darwinism on Philosophy" (1909). He held that Darwin's impact was to make "the principle of transition" the basis of all inquiry—not just biology, botany, and zoology, but epistemology and ethics as well. Darwinism jettisoned "absolute origins and absolute finalities" (as well as a prioris and a telos) from the theory of knowledge, demanding that modern inquirers "explore specific values and the specific conditions that generate them." Dewey recognized that abandoning all preformulated ideas about where scientific discoveries, claims to truth, and values should lead was a daunting challenge. But he preferred to advocate Darwinism as "philosophy that humbles" inquirers to actually test how their claims "work out in practice." "In having modesty forced upon it," Dewey averred, "philosophy also acquires responsibility."[4]

While John Dewey was still a high school student in Burlington, Vermont, in 1872, a group of Harvard researchers were beginning to feel those Darwinian influences at work on their ideas. The group, which called itself the Metaphysical Club, was organized by the logician Charles Sanders Peirce, and included the lawyer and future Supreme Court justice Oliver Wendell Holmes Jr., future Harvard professor of psychology and philosophy William James, and Chauncey Wright, a lecturer at Harvard whom the younger men referred to as their intellectual "boxing master."[5] Together they accepted the Darwinian account of the universe as one marked by contingencies and uncertainty and thus were determined to rethink ethics, truth, and meaning accordingly. They shared no strict doctrine on the meaning of truth, but rather a common conception of it as a tool human beings use as they make their way in the world. As a result, they came to regard truth claims and beliefs as nothing more than propositions that needed to be tested. Determined not to let any religious or scientific explanatory schemes sneak through on their credentials, the pragmatists insisted that *all* ideas must be certified by experience to be classified as true. James referred to this new philosophy as "pragmatism" (while Peirce preferred "pragmaticism" to distinguish his theory of truth from James's), which looked at truth by way of consequences, not origins, and by its practical results, not theory. The pragmatist philosophers believed that notions of mind and morals could no longer be based on timeless foundations, because, as they learned from Darwin, no such things existed.

William James, the first public face of pragmatism, also made a name for himself as one of the founders of the field of American psychology with his *Principles of Psychology* (1890). He brought his insights on human psychology to his work as a philosopher, which helped him to see that an individual's temperament, not just mind, played an important role in the making of her or his philosophical commitments. In his 1896 essay "The Will to Believe," James referred to this as one's *"passional nature,"* which steps in to make decisions when the individual is faced with a dilemma between positions for which there is insufficient evidence to resolve.[6] He saw how science and religion had become warring ideals that were particularly ferocious when their battleground moved from colleges and seminaries into the innermost reaches of an individual's conscience. Yet he believed that at the outermost reaches of both explanatory schemes awaited the promise of innovative new directions for modern research as well as creative possibilities for a meaningful life. Radically pluralist in his ethics and his epistemology, he stressed that there was no single account of the universe, only notions of truth that proved useful to the believer. James thus moved the study of religion away from dogmatics and focused instead on what he titled his magisterial work of 1902, "the varieties of religious experience."

James worked out his philosophy while teaching at Harvard and speaking on the American and European lecture circuit, and it was from a series of lectures that he produced his major work of philosophy, *Pragmatism: A New Name for Some Old Ways of Thinking* (1907). In it, he set out the dual role of pragmatism as both a method for coming to truth and a theory of truth. It was as hard to stick to as it was simple in conception: one is to get rid of abstractions, fixed principles, closed systems, dogmas, and foundations, replacing them with a testing of specific, concrete claims. It was to move from making philosophical assertions to examining how well they line up with actual human beings' actual experiences. James thus advocated a method to work out the truth in "*ambulando*, and not by any *a priori* definition."[7]

His theory of truth was really just a logical extension of this methodology. If one cannot say what truth is from the outset but must wait to see what proves itself to be true, then truth is just that: an idea that proves itself to be true. The result was a notion of truth that is contingent, perspectival, pluralist, and dynamic, so that truth changes from context to context, person to person, as well as over time. As James put it: "The trail of the human serpent is thus over everything. Truth independent; truth that we *find* merely; truth no longer malleable to human need; truth incorrigible, in a word; such truth exists indeed superabundantly ... but then it means only the dead heart of the living tree ... and may grow stiff with years of veteran service and petrified in men's regard by sheer antiquity." James regarded all truths to be "plastic": they are never absolute, but particular; they are not transcendent, but immanent in the daily workings of the world.[8]

From this the moral imperatives of pragmatism were clear: no one person, nation, religion, or scientific theory had a lock on truth. "Hands off," James challenged moderns in 1899, "neither the whole of truth nor the whole of good is revealed to any single observer . . . even prisons and sick-rooms have their special revelations." Pragmatist thought thus recommended to moderns an ethics so simple and straightforward and yet so difficult: one's truth can be one's truth "without presuming to regulate the rest of the vast field."[9]

Notwithstanding James's extraordinary philosophical range, it was John Dewey, the youngest of the first-generation pragmatists, whose ideas had the widest influence on twentieth-century American intellectual life. The sheer compass of Dewey's pragmatism (or what he called "instrumentalism") was extraordinary, addressing issues of logic, psychology, epistemology, moral philosophy, and aesthetics, as well as curriculum, educational policy, and social theory. He joined the newly founded University of Chicago in 1894, when the city was the scene of the dramatic social and economic dislocations of an uneven modernization. There he brought his theory of instrumental knowledge to bear on his desire for social reform through education by founding the Laboratory School in 1896. This experience helped launch his career-long effort to test his own philosophy in the everyday world of politics, art, and public life. His *Quest for Certainty* of 1929 offered a vigorous challenge to epistemological and ethical foundationalism, advancing the proposition that truths are no more, but also no less, than experimental efforts to enable human beings to purposefully negotiate a variable universe. What more useful proposition could there be for Americans to negotiate their own pluralistic, indeterminate, variable America? Dewey thus lived his own pragmatic gospel by encouraging modern intellectuals to dispense with the problems of philosophy and address themselves instead to the "problems of men."[10]

From Pragmatism to Progressivism

While James and Dewey recognized that pragmatism was a product of Darwinian thought, they also believed it could be used to conquer social problems underwritten by its offshoot—a dominant strand of social Darwinism, which accepted those problems as the unalterable facts of existence. Darwin considered the British philosopher Herbert Spencer's "social Darwinism" anathema and distanced himself from Spencer's advocacy of the "survival of the fittest" (a phrase Spencer invented and used to justify his laissez-faire economic and political ideas). Observers from all corners of American society could see that industrialization was a messy affair rife with bitter labor conflicts, extreme disparities in access and quality of education for children, poverty at one end of the economic spectrum and huge concentrations of wealth at the other, and cities polluted by unchecked industrial growth. But following Spencer's assurances, many people came to believe that the process of a modernizing America, tooth and claw as it seemed, was simply following the iron law of social development. They believed that the hardships, smut, and suffering were prices worth paying for progress.

The birth pangs of modernization at the turn of the century drew the attention of increasing numbers of educated, progressive, middle-class critics, who rejected the tenets of laissez-faire and survival of the fittest, as well as the nonexistent or ineffectual governmental oversight they produced. Highly educated in the most up-to-date academic research, progressives sought to merge scientific principles and practices of experimentation, organization, and efficiency for the moral betterment of society. Largely reformist, not radical in temperament, they did not seek to reject capitalism and industrial democracy but rather to root out its excesses and weaknesses. The vast majority of progressive reformers had grown up in racially and religiously homogenous small towns, and they longed for that sense of community and belonging in the bustling, anonymous modern city. Through their writings and their activism, they posed a counterforce to Gilded Age immoderation and fragmentation and provided a new narrative for modernization that could knit together immigrant groups and native-born Americans, the haves and have-nots, a thriving industry and a robust social democracy. An emerging reform-minded journalist and former student of William James at Harvard, Walter Lippmann, wrote the landmark text of progressivism, *Drift and Mastery: An Attempt to Diagnose the Current Unrest*, in 1914. Showing the close relation between pragmatist impulses and progressive desires, Lippmann stressed, "We can no longer treat life as something that has trickled down to us. We have to deal with it deliberately, devise its social organization, alter its tools, formulate its method, educate and control it."[11]

Though the reach of progressive reforms extended to rural communities, America's industrializing cities became the main focus of their energies as they turned university campuses, civic institutions, and urban streets into laboratories for social improvement. A most vivid embodiment of pragmatist thought and urban progressive action was one of America's foremost social reformers, Jane Addams, a pioneering social worker, activist, feminist, and pacifist. In 1889, together with her friend Ellen Gates Starr, she founded Hull House in Chicago, America's first social settlement. Hull House primarily drew educated, native-born, middle-class women, who came to live and work with Chicago's poor and immigrant communities. It offered a range of services, including day care for children, a library, employment assistance, classes in English and citizenship, and job training. Hull House reformers thus took seriously their work as urban scientists and the settlement house as a social laboratory.

Much like the Social Gospel and Christian Socialism of religious liberals and radicals of the same period, Addams maintained that progressive interventions would refashion economic, political, and public life to be more equitable, transparent, and just, while also transforming the individuals who worked within them. But Addams's work was not linked with a church (although she did view it as an expression of what she called the "renaissance of the early Christian humanitarianism"). Nor was it charity or philanthropy, both of which are unilateral acts of assistance, not reciprocal ones, and therefore underscore social and economic imbalances rather than remedy them. She described the impulse as a "coöperative ideal" of mutual assistance, a form of exchange more in line with a democracy of equals. If she sought a collaboration between America's haves and have-nots, it was only to foster the conditions that could help end this distinction. The path to social improvement was not simply being nice; it was to be a rigorous social scientist analyzing, testing, and implementing strategies that work. "We must learn to trust our democracy, giant-like and threatening as it may appear in its uncouth strength and untried applications," she wrote.[12] Both a good friend of and influence on John Dewey, Addams demonstrated how progressive reforms were an example of pragmatic testing of democratic ideals.

Progressive intellectuals were never content merely to observe social problems at a distance. Even those based at the university made regular ventures into city centers and rural communities to conduct fieldwork and gather data. Some carved out spaces for their work by founding independent "little magazines" and journals of opinion. Others frequented public libraries and labor halls by day and participated in makeshift "salons" and couch surfed in friends' apartments at night, as they scraped together a living from their writing. But as the proliferation of the extraordinary progressive social criticism of the period demonstrates, all proved to be invaluable sites from which to study the vibrancy of American life and to consider ways to close the gap between democratic theory and social practice.

The Politics of Cultural Pluralism

The untapped possibilities and the perils of American pluralism preoccupied some of the most influential early twentieth-century progressive intellectuals. It was at this time that many white, Protestant, propertied elites disparaged the influx of "unwashed" masses from Southern and Eastern Europe, and satirical magazines such as *Puck* and *The Wasp* circulated images of Irish laborers as apes and Chinese laborers as hordes of locusts. Somehow they had forgotten that once upon a time, their people were immigrants to America, too.

Opposing racial and ethnic chauvinism to embrace the "melting pot" (a phrase introduced to Americans in 1908 by Israel Zangwill's play of that name) would not be easy. It required persuasive arguments and evidence to challenge the social Darwinist and hierarchical thinking supporting the mainstream prejudices of the day. This was especially daunting as some of the most progressive American thinkers themselves harbored such chauvinisms. The pioneer sociologist and progressive advocate of workers' rights Edward A. Ross was also a flagrant racist who in the most prestigious scientific journals of the day warned against immigration for fear of Anglo Saxon "race suicide" (a term he coined in 1901).[13] It is no wonder that the philosopher and sociologist W. E. B. Du Bois, coming of age when Ross's ideas were at the height of both academic and popular fashion, maintained that "the problem of the Twentieth Century is the problem of the color-line," while lamenting the "double-consciousness" of the African American forced to "[look] at one's self through the eyes of others, of measuring one's soul by the tape of a world that looks on in amused contempt and pity."[14]

The German-born American anthropologist Franz Boas emerged as a crucial force working to undermine the authority of scientific racism. While still in Germany, he had written his dissertation using psychology and physics to understand perception of the color of water. This may not announce itself as a particularly momentous topic, but it turns out that for Boas, and for the field of anthropology he later entered, it was. In his study, he showed that the perception of water color is dependent on the viewer's standpoint, assumptions, and experience. In other words, color perception was context dependent, even learned, and was not innate in the viewer or in the properties of water. As he moved into the emerging field of anthropology, then a speculative discipline among its Victorian practitioners, Boas drew these insights from his training as a physicist and approached human cultures similarly as dynamic and situational. Rather than accept anthropology as a theoretical enterprise producing generalizations about a universal "culture," Boas turned to a group-specific, site-specific ethnography of "cultures" in an effort to make the "science of humans" a truly empirical enterprise. "Civilization," Boas stressed repeatedly over his long career, "is not something absolute, but ... it is relative."[15]

While university-sponsored research could help challenge racial prejudice, for a black woman like Ida B. Wells, born into slavery and with limited access to formal schooling, the strategies for the progressive struggle against racism looked quite different. Her medium was not scholarly books on ethnography but rather a pamphlet on the perversion of lynching, *A Red Record: Tabulated Statistics and Alleged Causes of Lynching in the United States, 1892-1893-1894* (1895). But like Boas, Wells turned to evidence rather than theories, and examples rather than generalizations, to debunk racist arguments. Hers was the first study to use statistical evidence to demonstrate how lynching had become a race-specific form of vigilantism. After the Civil War, the number of whites lynched fell precipitously, while the number of African Americans lynched increased dramatically, with an extraordinary 1,111 murdered by hanging between 1882 and 1894. Her choice to publish her material in pamphlet form was determined not by her lack of resources to publish it as a book, but by the fact that it could be produced cheaply on a wide scale. To change public opinion, she had to first create her public, which needed to include whites and blacks, people of means and those without.

As Boas's anthropology and Wells's statistical analyses show, the progressive agenda—to root out white Americans' squeamishness about diversity and to recognize it instead as the very feature that recommends American democracy to the world—came in a variety of forms. Understanding that the fight for diversity needed to open imaginations and encourage thoughtful reflection, the cultural critic Randolph Bourne stepped up to the challenge by crafting some of the most lyrical essays—and powerful arguments—of the progressive movement. Before his untimely death at the age of thirty-two in 1918, Bourne was widely celebrated as the professional spokesman and prophet of a new generation of young intellectuals. He had grown up despising the austere Presbyterianism and stifling Victorianism of his New Jersey middle-class upbringing. When he arrived in New York City to study at Columbia University in 1909, he felt that for the first time in his life, he "breathe[d] a larger air."[16] Within a few short years, the essays that flowed from his pen covered topics ranging from youth culture and friendship to university education and national and international politics. But it was his 1911 essay, "The Handicapped—By One of Them," that reveals Bourne steadying himself to take on the challenge of creating a more inclusive American culture, one less fearful of difference, whether it be cultural, racial, or physical. With a face misshaped by a botched forceps delivery, and hunchbacked and dwarfed from spinal tuberculosis at age four, Bourne, an outsider, had some sense of what it must feel like to be a new immigrant or black in America. It is to be always, invariably, "discounted at the start."[17]

During World War I, Bourne turned his sights to the belligerent nationalism and cramped nativism coursing through American society. With "Trans-National America" (1916), he skewered the provincialism of Anglo-Americans, unwilling or unable to recognize not just the moral bankruptcy but also the intellectual slackness of their arguments for immigration restrictions, Americanization campaigns, and Jim Crow. Even the "melting-pot" ideal, Bourne argued, was an outdated form of "forced chauvinism," for it took Anglo-Saxon culture as the measure against which all others needed to conform. "We are all foreign-born or the descendants of foreign-born, and if distinctions are to be made between us they should rightly be on some other ground than indigenousness." Bourne reminded his readers that "the early colonists did not come to be assimilated in an American melting-pot. They did not come to adopt the culture of the American Indian. . . . They came to get freedom to live as they wanted to." Already in 1916 he called for a "dual citizenship" not as an exception but as a basic fact of American identity. He saw this as preparation for a cosmopolitan "international citizenship," the likes of which would have helped Europe and the United States to avoid the calamity of an international war. Rediscovered as an inspirational, if romantic, blueprint for American multiculturalism in the second half of the century, Bourne's "Trans-National America" was, in fact, a study in hard-headed realism. "Let us face realistically the America we have around us. Let us work with the forces that are at work. Let us make something of this trans-national spirit instead of outlawing it. Already we are living this cosmopolitan America."[18]

Randolph Bourne died a month after the armistice, a victim of the global influenza pandemic of 1918–19. He did not live long enough to see America come down from its war hysteria, but he did live long enough to be devastated by its fury. He had been one of the very few progressive intellectuals who thought that the United States entering the war—even a "great" one—was a gross abandonment of pragmatist practices and progressive ideals. John Dewey, arguably the most prominent and influential intellectual in the period, thought otherwise. And where Dewey went with his support for American entry, so went a nation that just six months earlier voted President Wilson back into office as a reward for keeping them out of war.

During 1917, Bourne produced a series of fierce and stinging antiwar articles, skewering "War and the Intellectuals" and "The Collapse of American Strategy," and challenging the wisdom of his former Columbia professor and erstwhile intellectual hero Dewey, and Dewey's prowar progressive followers, in "Twilight of Idols." Bourne indicted Dewey for what he believed was his former mentor's wielding pragmatic instrumentalism instrumentally only, using it to concede power to the *is* of massive global conflict rather than to the *ought* of fostering global peace and more democratic values at home.

Bourne confessed to feeling "left in the lurch" by a philosophy that had so inspired other Americans to think themselves out of the narrow confines of inherited conventions and into a way of being in America—and the world—that appreciated difference while fostering understanding. It was indeed pragmatism that just a year earlier enabled him to dream of a pluralistic America that embraces its transnationality. The Bourne of 1917 was in no way proposing to scrap pragmatism, but to try for a pragmatism that recognizes that "vision must constantly outshoot technique."[19]

The response from fellow progressives, almost all of whom threw their support behind Wilson, was swift and punishing. Bourne's colleagues at the *New Republic* stopped publishing his pieces, the *Seven Arts* little magazine he helped found folded because one of its main financial backers was outraged by Bourne's antiwar stance, and *The Dial*, where he had served as editor, kicked him off the masthead. Only one thing rivaled the ferociousness of his fellow progressives' response: the coruscating passion, acumen, and beauty of Bourne's vision of a pluralistic, tolerant, and peaceful America, whose arguments against war are as relevant today as they were fearsome in 1917.

Chapter 6

Roots and Rootlessness: 1920–45

One of the goals of intellectual history is to try to access, as best we can, not simply the ideas but also the lived experiences of historical actors. The remarkable thing about the interwar period is that it is replete with commentators on American life who give us both in their work. Some were native born, and others arrived as exiles. Some welcomed the comforts of the technologies of the period, and others warned against their dangers. Some worked with prose, others with paint and photographs. But together they form a generation of articulate and incisive commentators who help us come in contact with the exciting but challenging moral worlds of interwar Americans.

In *This Side of Paradise* (1920), F. Scott Fitzgerald announced the postwar arrival of his "new generation . . . grown up to find all Gods dead, all wars fought, all faiths in man shaken."[1] It was the period when the vanguard anthropologist Margaret Mead compared the homogenous Samoan society with the mainland's stunted ability to grapple with its own pluralism: "[Americans] have many standards but we still believe that only one standard can be the right one."[2] This was the period in which African Americans responded to the vitriol and violence of a resurgent Ku Klux Klan with an equally intense fury harnessed by their verse. "I, too, sing America," wrote Langston Hughes in 1923, co-opting Walt Whitman's sanguine "I hear American singing" and tingeing it with acerbity and daring: "I am the darker brother. They send me to eat in the kitchen [w]hen company comes. . . . Tomorrow, I'll be at the table [w]hen company comes. Nobody'll dare [s]ay to me, 'Eat in the kitchen'. . . . They'll see how beautiful I am [a]nd be ashamed."[3] This is the period of the stock market crash and Great Depression, as well as prescient observers who warned of the moral bankruptcy underwriting the buoyant optimism of the 1920s. In 1929, even before the crash gave Americans reason to question their values, Walter Lippmann lamented that the "acids of modernity" were corroding Americans' moral compass.[4] Words like these are portals to the past, enabling us to feel the inner sting of Americans' consciences and to see postwar America through their eyes.

This period from the end of World War I to the end of World War II was marked by intellectual daring and profound antimodernism. The Roaring Twenties bellowed not only with new insights into human nature and experiments in modernist poetry, art, and literature but also with fears about loose sexual mores, racial mongrelization, and deicide. In the aftermath of victory in World War I, American thinkers from diverse backgrounds and viewpoints participated in a common, and by now long-standing, project of finding new terms and modes of expression for explaining America to itself. Whether condemning American commercialization, trying to understand the causes and implications of the Great Depression, or rethinking democratic foundations amidst the growing specter of totalitarianism in Europe, they examined America's unfinished revolution for freedom and equality and provided new inspiration for finding unity in its diversity.

The Shadows of Modernization

In the years after World War I, national and international economic and social developments pushed and pulled Americans in different, sometimes opposing, directions. On the one side were the forces of modernization—new scientific theories, new technologies for the home, and new ideas about family and sexuality—all making new ways of thinking, living, and loving possible. On the other side was the pull of tradition—religious revivals, the familiarity of one's hometown in a period of migration and urbanization, and old fears and animosities—tugging at many Americans' minds and hearts. But there was one thing both those looking to the future for confidence and those looking to the past for comfort had in common. They could agree that the flow of history into which they were inexorably pulled was producing profound transformations to their America as well as their sense of their place within it. Their world, whether they liked it or not, was quickly becoming very different from the one into which they were born.

The forces of modernization in American life were everywhere apparent. Extraordinary postwar economic growth, thanks to increased industrial production and corporate profitability, a rising per capita income, and a growing number of Americans getting comfortable buying goods and services on credit, brought seismic changes in daily life. Labor-saving devices such as electric refrigerators, washing machines, and vacuum cleaners allowed for more leisure time than ever before. The phonograph, the radio, and the "talkies" kept people entertained during that leisure time. Old cities were made new thanks to electrification, while a modern kind of living in something called "the suburbs" became available on the outskirts of those cities thanks to the automobile. New print technologies allowed for greater production of mass-marketed books and magazines, passing along new trends in fashion, culture, and thought. The period was also one of self-described "new"-ness, with the liberated "New Negro" and "New Woman" as modern social types ready to make larger claims on the public sphere. The ratification of the Nineteenth Amendment in 1920, giving women the right to vote, was an extraordinary breakthrough for feminists who sought equality with men. But the "New Woman" quickly became less associated with a female at the ballot box and more linked to the chopped-haired, painted-faced, kittenish flapper. With a cigarette in hand, this modern woman waved goodbye to traditional notions of femininity and propriety.

If the 1920s seemed to be a go-go decade, there were also many American observers who just wanted its modernizing forces to stop. The United States had won the war, but some Americans felt that victory culture brought with it decadence, profligacy, and too many strange foreigners with unfamiliar customs ill-fitting the sort of community they longed for. Warren G. Harding ran for president in 1920 promising "normalcy." Given that he was the first politician to so use the word, he had all the latitude he wanted to define it rather vaguely as "a regular steady order of things. I mean normal procedure, the natural way, without excess."[5] Over the course of the 1920s, however, a series of events helped give the term more precision. Normalcy came to mean isolationism, with the United States backing away from the League of Nations. Normalcy came to mean antiradicalism, with the Bolshevik Revolution of November 1917 and labor unrest at home bringing on fears of communism and anarchism. For many old-stock white Protestants, normalcy also came to mean a belligerent nativism with tightened immigration laws (the Emergency Quota Act of 1921 and the National Origins Act of 1924), as well as growing membership in a bigger, badder Ku Klux Klan (KKK), which now lengthened its list of enemies to include Jews and Catholics in addition to African Americans. The quest for normalcy tracked with growing fears about "foreign thinkers" slipping into school curricula and polluting American students' morality. The Scopes "Monkey" Trial helped yoke Darwinism to Satanism and helped give rise to fundamentalism, a new development that had profound consequences for Christianity in the twentieth-century United States. And now with the growing popularity of Sigmund Freud's ideas about the dark inner workings of moderns' minds and libidos, the Austrian psychiatrist joined Karl Marx and Friedrich Nietzsche to form an unholy trinity of continental thinkers corrupting American thought.

The tug of war between modern and traditional forces proved most destabilizing, however, when they competed for supremacy within the mind of a single intellectual. A prime example is the growing faith in eugenics: the use of "advanced" sciences as apologias for racial and ethnic exclusion. Margaret Sanger, the sex educator who opened the first birth control clinic in the United States and advocated tirelessly for women's rights to self-determination, represented the pinnacle of the modern, advanced woman. She was also an ethnic chauvinist—a stance perfectly in keeping with conventional prejudices of her day, though from the vantage point of today, a seemingly odd fit with her extremely unconventional ideas about sexuality. In *Woman and the New Race* (1920), she understood that "voluntary motherhood implies a new morality." That in no way meant, however, that she wanted "foreigners who have come in hordes [and] have brought with them their ignorance of hygiene" to be free to make their own reproductive choices.[6] In *The Pivot of Civilization* (1922), Sanger described "science [as] the ally" in limiting the procreation of the "unfit" and "feeble-minded."[7]

Sanger's views of African Americans, Southern Europeans, and Asians were not as extreme as those of Lothrop Stoddard, a Harvard-trained American historian and prominent eugenicist and racial theorist. And yet it was his authoritative studies of the "colored" threat to the white race, most notably *The Rising Tide of Color against White World-Supremacy* (1920) and *The Revolt against Civilization: The Menace of the Underman* (1922), that recommended him as an ideal authority to serve on Sanger's American Birth Control League's national council and to publish articles in the *Birth Control Review*. Stoddard helped confirm in the minds of many Americans that "race is not an abstract theory; it is a concrete fact, which can be accurately determined by scientific tests."[8] Both Sanger and Stoddard represent the seamless intellectual extension of nineteenth-century scientific racism into interwar eugenic theory, as both used the authority of modern science to credentialize racial bigotry.

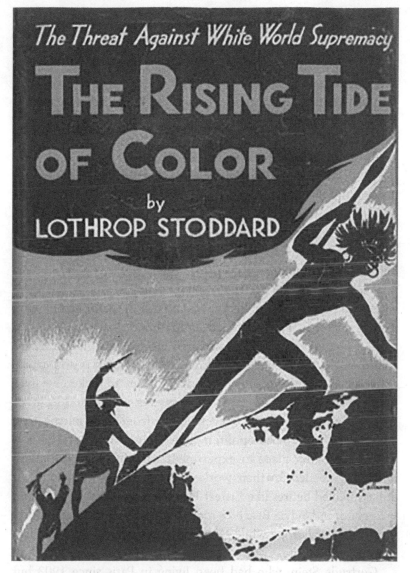

Lothrop Stoddard's *The Rising Tide of Color* (1920) was one of the most influential works of racial forecasting in the 1920s. Stoddard's text provided a "racial map of the globe," showing how the population of the "colored" world outnumbered the "white" world two to one, and warned against immigration and miscegenation as the greatest threats to white Americans. *University of Wisconsin–Madison, Special Collections*

From the Lost Generation to the Founding
of an African American Renaissance

Ezra Pound moved to London in 1908 at the age of twenty-three, attracted to its intellectual energy and aesthetic experimentation. He lectured on medieval poetry, wrote criticism, served as the foreign editor for the Chicago-based *Poetry* magazine, and exchanged laughter and barbs with the Fabian Socialists George Bernard Shaw and H. G. Wells, painter Wyndham Lewis, and philosopher Bertrand Russell. But the war dealt his enthusiasm a punishing blow. Pound recoiled in horror as he watched his generation of young men become psychologically and physically ravaged—if not killed—for a ruinous nationalism, for a grotesque conception of patriotism, and for politicians' ambitions and businessmen's greed. He captured his fury and heartache in his 1920 poem "Hugh Selwyn Mauberley," lamenting that the best of his generation had died "for an old bitch gone in the teeth, [f]or a botched civilization."[9]

Not long after Pound documented his devastation and disenchantment, a number of his fellow American writers and artists who shared his disillusionment fled to Europe to make new lives for themselves. No European country was wholly innocent or spared the ravages of war. Nevertheless, from their perspective, Europe was more cosmopolitan than their provincial America, and thus a better place to experiment with the way of life and ideas they needed for their work. The strong postwar American dollar enabled figures like Ernest Hemingway, T. S. Eliot, F. Scott Fitzgerald, and Sylvia Beach to make a life among the new literary modernists of Europe while rejecting the persistent Victorianism of American culture.

Gertrude Stein, who had been living in Paris since 1903 but welcomed the postwar rush of American talent to her adopted homeland, referred to these American prodigals and pilgrims as a "lost generation." She did not intend this as a hearty endorsement of intellectual vagabondage, but rather as a way of poking fun at their wild ways and youthfulness and to suggest, in a more serious sense, that they were searching for some existential anchors that they would never find. In her view, they were lost metaphysically. Hemingway was the first to grab on to this designation, seeing it as a fitting moniker for expatriate Americans' intellectual restlessness and yearning. If they were homeless minds, then better to find temporary shelter among the ruins of Europe than in an American intellectual and cultural wasteland.

While a generation of young, white writers and artists welcomed being lost, that same generation of young, black writers and artists wanted nothing more than to find themselves in an America they could comfortably call "home." Confronting persistent racism in the face of a revived KKK and in nineteenth-century evolutionary theories repurposed to support twentieth-century Jim Crow segregation and imperialism, a growing number of African American poets, playwrights, painters, and essayists went about fighting American prejudice by first finding themselves a history to connect them from the present to their American (and before that African) past. What became known as the Harlem (or Negro) Renaissance was an extraordinary flowering of black intellectual production in the 1920s and 1930s, which sought heightened racial consciousness and pride, as well as interracial unity.

There was no one theme, aesthetic, or voice that defined the movement, though Howard University philosopher Alain Locke's *The New Negro* of 1925 gave it a mission and an identity. Locke was the first African American to win a Rhodes scholarship, and he studied with philosophers Josiah Royce and Horace Kallen, receiving his PhD from Harvard in 1918. He had made a name for himself through his "critical relativism," where he took the pluralism undergirding pragmatism and extended it into his own form of radical racial and cultural theory. Those commitments can be seen in his introduction to the collection, where he takes on the "fiction" of racial essentialism behind the "much asserted rising tide of color" while recognizing that African Americans needed to come up with new intellectual and aesthetic terms for self-definition and self-determination. Fostering racial pride need not encourage racial absolutism or divisions. On the contrary, progressive race thinking, cognizant of the relativism of different cultures and groups, was a way to see the value and beauty of each of them, both comparatively and in and of themselves. Drawing on diasporic and Zionist discourses, Locke argued that worldwide persecution of black people, like Jewish people, was "making the Negro international," and he described Harlem, the vibrant hub of African American artistic experimentation, as the "home of the Negro's 'Zionism.'"[10]

The Renaissance writers' and artists' ideas, aesthetics, and arguments did not move in lockstep with one another. Yet they all reveal a shared desire to devise their own measure of aesthetic and intellectual value through artistic experimentation and new terms for their black identity. For W. E. B. Du Bois, that meant dispensing with the question he posed in *The Souls of Black Folk*—"how does it feel to be a problem?"—and recognizing it as nothing more than a confession of white racial anxiety.[11] In the years leading up to and during this florescence, Du Bois organized the first Pan-African Congress in Paris in 1919, helping to provide a diasporic focus to the movement; published *Darkwater: Voices from within the Veil* (1920) and *The Gift of Black Folk: The Negroes in the Making of America* (1924); and even experimented with fiction with his 1928 novel, *Dark Princess: A Romance*.

The ethnographer and folklorist Zora Neale Hurston combined her personal experiences growing up in an all-black Florida town and her training with Alain Locke at Howard University and anthropologist Franz Boas at Barnard College to produce her masterpiece, *Their Eyes Were Watching God* (1937), which promoted pride in the customs and folkways of Southern rural blacks. The poetry of the movement likewise sought to find the beauty and particularity of African Americans' experience. Roughly a century before the New Negro movement, Ralph Waldo Emerson affirmed in "The Poet" that "it is not metres, but a metre-making argument, that makes a poem."[12] It is hard to think of better examples of Emersonian poets than Langston Hughes, Claude McKay, Countee Cullen, and James Weldon Johnson, who blended impassioned criticism and gorgeous lyricism in their verse.

While they looked to Africa to imagine their distant pasts, as well as to blacks in the diaspora to create a movement with global reach, the contributors to the Harlem Renaissance wanted, above all, to make America a place they could call "home." Although it is difficult to trace the efficacy of their efforts in turning antiblack bigotry and fear into a durable racial solidarity and inclusion, it is much easier to see how, even with the barriers to freedom of Jim Crow, Renaissance artists and intellectuals reimagined their belonging in America.

Intellectual Underpinnings of the New Deal

The shock and devastation brought on by the stock market crash of 1929 and the subsequent depression created an urgency to understand American life in the past, as well as its prospects for the future. Perhaps this helps explain why the phrase "the American dream" was popularized in 1930, a moment in history when Americans were haunted by their worst nightmares. It was James Truslow Adams's *The Epic of America* (1931) that first promoted the notion of "the American dream" not only as a guiding vision through the centuries of American history but also as a universal aspiration: "that dream of a land in which life should be better and richer and fuller for every man, with opportunity for each according to his ability or achievement."[13] It is hard to believe that these words were written and, moreover, that they inspired such widespread fidelity during a period when a severe drought was scorching the earth and brutalizing farmers on the Great Plains, when six million Americans were unemployed, and when breadlines and food riots cropped up all over American cities. Aspirational histories like Adams's were good for

As if in direct response to the collector of Africana Arthur Schomburg's claim that "the American Negro must remake his past in order to make his future," New Negro Renaissance artist Loïs Mailou Jones's *The Ascent of Ethiopia* (1932) presents an allegory of American black experience, emerging from its African past, moving through slavery and liberation, and finding its fullest expression in the Harlem Renaissance. *Milwaukee Art Museum, Purchase, African American Art Acquisition Fund, matching funds from Suzanne and Richard Pieper, with additional support from Arthur and Dorothy Nelle Sanders, M 1993.19. Photographer: John R. Glembin. With permission of Loïs Mailou Jones Trust*

giving Depression-era Americans hope. But what they needed as well was the help of American thinkers.

Intellectuals found this opportunity to directly help their fellow Americans in Franklin Delano Roosevelt's New Deal reforms. Roosevelt thought that nothing less than "bold, persistent experimentation" could work to repair a devastated economy and desperate society.[14] He recruited a variety of economists, social scientists, and legal scholars to work as governmental advisers, believing that knowledge was the best weapon against economic and social disrepair. Almost no domain of American life was out of the reach of New Deal programs' scientific investigation and administration. Though imperfect and uneven in their handling of Americans' basic needs, the programs focused on everything from the unemployed, the sick, and the elderly to home loans, soil erosion, bank deposits, and rural electrification.

While the New Dealers believed all areas of social and economic concern should fall within their purview, there was, at least, one idea they wanted to see forever pushed to the margins of American thought: rugged individualism. According to Charles Beard, America's foremost historian of the period, the exaltation of the antisocial, individualistic, "frontier" mentality described by Frederick Jackson Turner roughly forty years earlier had become dangerously passé. "The cold truth," Beard averred, "is that the individualist creed of everybody for himself and the devil take the hindmost is principally responsible for the distress in which Western civilization finds itself. . . . Whatever merits the creed may have had in days of primitive agriculture and industry, it is not applicable in an age of technology, science, and rationalized economy."[15]

The new optimism that intellectuals were not just dreamy-eyed perseverators but discerning and determined problem solvers turned up in the terminology of the period. "Brains Trust," a term coined by a *New York Times* reporter who observed the increased role of academic intellectuals in important governmental roles, became one of the most notable phrases of the New Deal. The term initially referred to Raymond Moley, Rexford G. Tugwell, and Adolf Berle Jr., Columbia University professors who advised Roosevelt on economic policy and helped establish regulatory solutions to the country's economic problems, but it came into wider use to describe the sudden bumper crop of professional intellectuals in political roles. Though their area of research expertise varied widely, they all shared a similar revulsion with abstractions and an insistence on the practical applications and verifiability of ideas and theories. According to Tugwell, an economist, "conceptualism is the particular bugbear of the social sciences," adding that work of the social scientist "in the fields and factories" is akin to what the natural scientist does in the laboratory.[16] Many of the New Deal reformers, who got their start in the pre–World War I progressive reform initiatives, carried with them their convictions that scientific inquiry and administration were crucial for remedying social problems. Frances Perkins, the secretary of labor and main visionary behind the minimum wage, Social Security, and universal health insurance, drew on her own experiences working at Hull House in Chicago.

The New Deal programs also exhibited an appreciation for what writers and artists could do to bind up the country's wounds. The Works Progress Administration (later renamed the Work Projects Administration [WPA]) initiated a number of programs for unemployed art critics, teachers, librarians, folklorists, novelists, and playwrights to go into the American "field" and retrieve people's ways of life, all in an effort to draw out the grit and goodness of the American "folk," even in times of great distress. Many writers contributed to *The American Guide* series (1937–41) with essays on the culture, lifestyles, history, and geography of different states, balancing a romantic nationalism with a celebration of regional diversity and particularity. An even more extraordinary and visionary undertaking was the systematic effort to interview African American men and women who had been born into slavery and still lived to testify to this darker side of the American experience. In addition, a veritable army of artists was hired to help cultivate an aesthetic for the nation. Artists designed posters, painted murals on public buildings, installed statues in city centers, and taught community art classes, making the 1930s one of the most vibrant eras of public art in American history. Many WPA artists and art historians also helped with a massive project, the Index of American Design, which documented the crafts and decorative arts in America from the colonial period to 1900. This was no study in quaint antiquarianism, but a document produced by forward-looking modern artists searching for a usable past.

Despite garnering the support and appreciation of a majority of Americans, Roosevelt and his New Deal programs did inspire their fair share of outraged critics. The governor of Louisiana, Huey Long, made a national name for himself breaking his one-time support for Roosevelt and challenging his initiatives, which he saw as too subservient to the demands and desires of corporations and the wealthy. He offered instead his "Share Our Wealth" plan, which proposed to expropriate the wealth of the richest and redistribute it to the poor in the form of a $5,000 homestead and an annual income of $2,500. Roosevelt had an equally threatening enemy in the Michigan-based Catholic priest and radio personality Father Charles Coughlin, who ratcheted up the worry of his forty-five million largely white, working-class listeners into a full-scale panic with his anticommunist, anticapitalist, rabidly anti-Semitic diatribes, as he called for a "Christian front" to fight off these forces of evil. Because the hyperbole and hysteria of Long's and Coughlin's rhetoric exhibited more rancor and resentment than reasoned arguments, piecing together their logic is not easy. Nevertheless, they helped inspire sincere dread among their followers that the modern industrial state was horning in on their personal autonomy and trampling on precious liberties.

Intellectual Exiles Arrive in America

One of the most important events in twentieth-century American intellectual and cultural life was the massive immigration of German-speaking intellectuals, artists, and scientists fleeing Nazism in the 1930s and early 1940s. The refugees brought with them their erudition, training, and, in some cases, international reputations in the arts and sciences, and they had an enormous influence on American academic and cultural institutions. The refugee intellectuals included, among others, Albert Einstein, Thomas Mann, Berthold Brecht, Arnold Schoenberg, Karen Horney, Walter Gropius, Franz Neumann, Ernst Cassirer, Theodor Adorno, Herbert Marcuse, Eric Voegelin, Wilhelm Reich, Erik Erikson, Paul Tillich, and Fritz Lang. Reading this list of extraordinary talent makes it easy to see why Walter W. S. Cook, director of the Institute of Fine Arts at New York University, called Hitler his "best friend": "[Hitler] shakes the tree and I collect the apples."[17]

The bulk of the intellectuals arrived in America during the 1930s, a period marked by political isolationism, anti-immigrant nativism, and economic depression. Many were rejected by universities and colleges that closed ranks to keep out Jews and foreigners. But a number of savvy university administrators recognized that they could benefit from their fame and expertise, especially as many American academic institutions were still trying to establish themselves internationally. In addition, the new crop of highly trained social scientists was seen as a valuable research resource for the development and administration of New Deal programs. And last, and perhaps most important, the émigrés' firsthand experience with Nazism gave them the insights and moral authority to comment on the consequences of European totalitarian regimes for Americans.

German refugee intellectuals understood profoundly the ramifications of living in a totalitarian state and became invaluable commentators on the regime they had fled. The political social scientist Franz Neumann's *Behemoth* (1942) was one of the first efforts to examine the economic, political, and social structures of National Socialism, and it provided a Marxist analysis of Nazism that argued for the primacy of economic motivations. Psychoanalyst Erich Fromm explored the social and psychological origins of totalitarianism, arguing that Nazism represented a retreat from the psychic burden and alienation of individual freedom. Protestant theologian Paul Tillich examined the loss of religion as one of the causes for the modern anxiety that culminated in the Holocaust, while political thinker Hannah Arendt directed her attention to the nationalist and political sources of Nazism. And novelist Thomas Mann wrote his *Joseph and His Brothers* tetralogy under "the shadow of Hitler," with the last volume, *Joseph the Provider*, about his new adopted homeland. It featured a Joseph influenced by Mann's "personal acquaintance with Franklin Roosevelt" and his "view of Joseph's administration in Egypt" bearing, as he put it, "traces of my impression of the New Deal."[18] The horrors of Nazi Germany, which were never exiled from his mind, became the setting for Mann's modern adaptation of the Faust myth in his dark and haunting *Doctor Faustus* (1947).

Much of the social and political theory in postwar America would extend from the contributions of refugee scholars. In the ensuing years, the émigrés' theories of mass society became widely read and popularized as Americans sought to comprehend the dynamics of Cold War geopolitics abroad and observed dangerous mass tendencies hiding behind atomistic individualism at home. Liberal sociologists in the 1950s and later a younger generation of counterculture critics in the 1960s discovered in the émigrés' works valuable theories for analyzing the alienation and conformism caused by the dominance of corporate bureaucracies and suburbanization in postwar American life. Thus, the mass emigration of European intellectuals in the 1930s and 1940s had dramatic long-term effects on the shaping of American thought in the postwar period.

The outbreak of war in Europe in 1939 had not snuck up on American intellectuals as the outbreak of war in Europe in 1914 had done; nevertheless, it alarmed them deeply and pressed them to rethink their roles as policy experts, political analysts, and cultural critics. Many lent their support to President Roosevelt, who campaigned in 1939 for an unprecedented third term promising neutrality. And many continued their support as he and his administration began to realize that being a neutral "arsenal of democracy" was untenable. For the United States' most prominent intellectuals, the Japanese bombing of Pearl Harbor in December 1941 snuffed out any ambiguity about America's obligation to defend its citizens, protect its allies, and keep the world as safe for democracy as possible. It also clarified American intellectuals' own responsibility to foster a collective commitment to democratic institutions and values.

Throughout the war, many Americans spoke in terms of the "public interest" and "democratic community" while too often overlooking or simply being blind to the ways in which their national institutions, like Jim Crow and Japanese internment camps, belied their inclusive rhetoric. But after the war was over, observers of American life recovered their temerity to call out the persistent gaps between America's democratic rhetoric and its undemocratic practices and find new ways to close them.

Chapter 7

The Opening of
the American Mind: 1945–70

Today's commentators typically view postwar American intellectual life as a period of staid traditionalism, stifling uniformity, complacency, and consensus. This reputation is surely warranted. Almost seamlessly, World War II transitioned into the Cold War between the United States and the Soviet Union, which brought intense polarization of American domestic politics, a nervous but belligerent jockeying for hegemony abroad, and a frightening and escalating arms race. The Cold War ushered in a second and even more widespread and feverish Red Scare with it, including loyalty oaths, the House Un-American Activities Committee, the McCarran Internal Security Act, the John Birch Society, and Senator Joseph McCarthy terrorizing Americans about "enemies from within." This was a period when, if the color of an American's skin was too dark or his or her sexual orientation too ambiguous, he or she could be accused of breaching national security. The pressure for a smooth, agreeable sameness also extended into American consumer culture. Unprecedented affluence and an ever-expanding culture of consumerism enabled more and more Americans to move into cookie-cutter Cape Cod–style suburban homes, to read the same lifestyle magazines and mass-market paperback novels, to slip into the same ready-to-wear cardigans and loafers, and to watch the same television shows while eating the same TV dinners set atop the same TV tray tables.

While policing and paranoia marked so much of this period—and the Cold War is the appropriate framing for understanding mid-twentieth-century American thought—viewing it only through this frame risks flattening the vibrant intellectual impulses at work at the time. The 1950s and early 1960s saw not only intellectual suffocation but also efforts to widen Americans' intellectual horizons. The dramatic expansion of higher education, think tanks, and the print culture marketplace; initiatives to create a lively conservative tradition; and the growing American interest in intellectual movements and spiritual practices from around the world all contributed to the opening of midcentury American thought, helping Americans (to use the words of Randolph Bourne) "breathe a larger air."

The Postwar Expansion of Intellectual Opportunity

America's new status as global superpower stimulated the development of its intellectual and cultural institutions at a pace and in a scale unprecedented in its history. With the massive postwar investment in higher education, the proliferation of intellectual institutes and artistic foundations, and the continued growth of federal agencies in need of policy experts and political analysts, intellectuals had opportunities for institutional affiliation as never before. American intellectual life became nothing short of a growth industry, and so too did intellectuals' interest in assessing the promises of these new alignments for American society.

American thinkers welcomed the opportunity to reassess their views of American intellectual culture and their place in it. A 1952 *Partisan Review* symposium devoted itself to the intellectual "reaffirmation and rediscovery of America."[1] With guarded optimism, contributors including Margaret Mead, Lionel Trilling, Sidney Hook, and Reinhold Niebuhr recognized that the experience of the Depression and war had chastened Americans, making them take notice of the valuable insights of intellectuals. Surveying recent history, Lionel Trilling noted with some astonishment that "for the first time in the history of the modern American intellectual, America is not to be conceived of as *a priori* the vulgarest and stupidest nation of the world."[2] *Time* magazine's June 11, 1956, article "America and the Intellectual: The Reconciliation," with a portrait of the cultural and intellectual historian Jacques Barzun and the lamp of learning burning brightly on the cover, captured the widespread feeling that a truce was in order.

But the opening of American thought extended beyond professional intellectuals and into wide-scale efforts to democratize intellectual life. A distinctive feature of the period is the widespread belief that a stable democracy required an educated citizenry, and proper education required extensive funding and a robust infrastructure. During the war, educators had seized on President Roosevelt's affirmation that "books are weapons in the war of ideas."[3] The Council on Books in Wartime distributed 122 million of their Armed Services Editions, paperbacks of major works of nonfiction, fiction, and even poetry, which helped rouse many soldiers' intellectual curiosity and yearning. The council reprinted classics like Plato's *Republic*, Mary Shelley's *Frankenstein*, Robert and Elizabeth Barrett Browning's *Love Poems*, and Walter Lippmann's *U.S. Foreign Policy* and turned F. Scott Fitzgerald's long-forgotten *The Great Gatsby* into the Great American novel. Thanks to these editions, soldiers could be enchanted with Whitman's poetry and be swept away by the mystical philosophy of the Lebanese American poet Kahlil Gibran. Those same GIs then came home to the Servicemen's Readjustment Act (or "GI Bill") of 1944, which provided, among other resources, educational subsidies for millions of returning servicemen to go to college.

After the war, the expansion of intellectual resources kept pace with the booming economy. Fierce competition in commercial publishing led to a dramatic increase in mass-market paperbacks. The National Defense Education Act passed in 1958 provided federal subsidies to libraries and higher education, which in turn opened up huge markets for textbook publishers. Even primary and secondary schoolers benefited from this surge of collective will and resources, with expenditures on public schools more than doubling between 1945 and 1950.

Postwar Political Commentary: Left, Right, and "Vital Center"

Given the extensive new opportunities for intellectual access, support, and employment, describing this period of American intellectual life as an "opening" makes sense. Describing it as all sunshine and light, though, does not. Long after the war, American intellectuals were still trying to come to terms with its devastations, which were the result of human choice and action, not natural disasters. This left many people wondering which aspects of the "Western intellectual tradition" (a phrase coined in the early twentieth century), if any, still had integrity, and which had proven themselves utterly inadequate for guiding moderns in the twentieth century. Suddenly progressive and New Deal–era reformers' sanguine notions of human progress seemed naïve, even a bit taunting. In the words of one historian of the period, "Never before had progress seemed so fragile, history so harmful or so irrelevant, science so lethal, aggregations of power so ominous, life so full of contingencies, human relationships so tenuous, the self so frail, man so flawed."[4]

A common concern animating postwar debates was how Americans should root and nourish a common democratic culture. While many intellectuals and educators could agree about the potential perniciousness of science and technology absent any clear moral vision guiding them, they struggled to find a shared language for what that vision—and those values—should be. In his 1959 essay "Two Cultures," the British scientist and novelist C. P. Snow lamented that the "intellectual life of the whole of western society" was divided between two very different frames of mind: the literary, or humanistic, and the scientific. Though he admitted that his warnings about the disturbing consequences of this "gulf of mutual incomprehension" were a little overdrawn, with regard to the tensions in 1950s American intellectual life, the characterization most definitely fit.[5] Different views on the methods of political and ethical inquiry were not the only thing dividing thinkers. More important was the question of what intellectual and moral foundations could support American collective life.

Pragmatism fell on hard times after the war, and it was no longer the promising peacemaker between competing intellectual impulses it was earlier in the century. Intellectuals and educators wanted more assurances about moral universals than pragmatism could give, and they took aim at the pragmatist notion that all truths are nothing more than provisional tools that help people navigate their complex worlds. As John Dewey remained the most prominent face of philosophical pragmatism up through—and even after—his death in 1952, it was his defense of an experimental approach to democratic politics that came under the most heated attacks. This was nothing new to Dewey as he had to continually explain and defend his instrumentalism in education, public policy, and private ethics throughout his long career. But the upbraiding was particularly damaging when it came from formidable thinkers like the theologian, philosopher, and political commentator Reinhold Niebuhr, who shared Dewey's desire for "a common faith" for political life, but not what he regarded as Dewey's naïve naturalism. Niebuhr thought Deweyian atheistic empiricism overpromised in its assumptions about the power of human intelligence and clarity of will. Describing himself as a "Christian realist," he insisted that "the recalcitrant forces in the historical drama have a power and persistence beyond our reckoning."[6]

Though Niebuhr and Dewey had long wrestled over the scope and limits of human power to foster a just and sustainable democracy, both were working firmly within a liberal framework. The liberalism that animated their thinking was an inheritance from the early nineteenth century, when the term first entered transatlantic discourse to pull together individual liberty, property rights, and democratic institutions to secure them. It drew on Locke's vision of a smoothly functioning civil society as a social contract between rational individual actors, as well as Adam Smith's principle that markets unfettered from state control operate with maximum efficiency and for the greatest benefits to all. In its Progressive era and New Deal iterations, liberal thinkers and politicians had put a higher premium on the role of the government—not to control the economy, but to manage it with knowledgeable experts redressing imbalances and weaknesses in it. Enlightened governance on behalf of the public good and safeguards to protect the disenfranchised took precedence over individual property rights. With the rise of Nazism and fascism in Europe, American liberalism re-emphasized Lockean tolerance for diversity as a core feature of open democratic societies in order to distinguish itself from iron-curtained totalitarian ones.

Both World War II and now a fierce Cold War daunted leading liberal intellectuals, causing them to find the weak spots in their vision of a vibrant liberalism in the charged and dangerous postwar world. But liberal intellectuals like historians Richard Hofstadter and Daniel Boorstin, economist John Kenneth Galbraith, literary critics Mary McCarthy and Alfred Kazin, and sociologists Daniel Bell and Patrick Moynihan did so not to topple liberalism, but to shore up its ruins. When they jabbed American liberal theories with charges of parochialism and facile optimism, they never doubted that, as political scientist Louis Hartz put it in 1955, the "liberal tradition in America," in some form or another, was the defining feature of American history and should remain so in the future.[7]

There were nevertheless some intellectual holdouts who begged to differ more fundamentally. Feeling exasperated with what they considered to be a smugness and complacency in midcentury liberals' worldview, a growing number of political and cultural critics identified themselves as "conservatives" offering an alternative.

Though the United States, unlike the United Kingdom or Canada, never had a "conservative" party, conservatism, they contended, did have an American history. They thus worked to sketch out a lost tradition, to persuade Americans to recognize it as their own, and to welcome it as a political term of self-understanding.

In quick succession, three books defining American conservatism appeared, providing momentum for critics who wanted to challenge what they saw as the prevailing orthodoxy of a glib liberalism. The views expressed in Peter Viereck's *Conservatism Revisited* (1949), William F. Buckley Jr.'s *God and Man at Yale* (1951), and Russell Kirk's *The Conservative Mind* (1953) did not always seamlessly line up with one another. Indeed, the elder Viereck identified the young Buckley as "Paul-in-a-hurry [who] skips the prerequisite of first being a rebel Saul" and distinguished his "shallow" campus conservativism from a "profound" one. Buckley offered an "easy booster affirmation that precedes the dark night of the soul" but not "the hard-won, tragic affirmation that follows it."[8] But together these and a growing number of prominent conservative commentators challenged to varying degrees the assumptions of midcentury liberalism by stressing the virtues of individualism over collectivism, capitalism over all forms of economic collectivism, hierarchy and order over egalitarianism, and caution over experimentalism as the "conservative way[s] to freedom."[9] They recognized that a political and intellectual movement, to get moving, needed media outlets to spread its gospel. With that in mind, Buckley founded the *National Review* in 1955 and Kirk the *Modern Age* in 1957 to rival liberal magazines such as the *New Republic, Atlantic Monthly*, and *Harper's*.

Liberals' and conservatives' visions of postwar democracy and the routes to it differed sharply; nevertheless, they could agree on a few things. First was their shared interest in—and ambivalence about—the European Enlightenment. The modifier "European" here is significant, because during this Cold War period it becomes necessary in order to distinguish it from a newly discovered "American" one. American historian Adrienne Koch was the first to

popularize the notion of a distinctly American (and more whole-
some) Enlightenment with a series of books on the founding fathers. According to Koch, "Th[eirs] is not the voice of absolute
idealism or doctrinaire liberalism" one sees in eighteenth-century
Europe, "but rather the voice of cautious, deliberative, and reasonable pragmatic wisdom."[10] The European Enlightenment also
captured the attention of Marxist German exiles Max Horkheimer
and Theodor Adorno, who looked to it to understand the origins of
modernity in *Dialectic of Enlightenment* (1944). They argued that the
Enlightenment *philosophes*, with their enthusiasm for "instrumental"
rationality, and their view that nothing is beyond human compre-
hension and the will to dominate, had laid the groundwork for the
"administered world" of Nazism. Adorno and Horkheimer were not
ones to mince words. As they put it: "Enlightenment is totalitarian."[11]
Such an extreme thought would have never occurred to conservative
commentators on the other end of the political spectrum. But Russell
Kirk, expressing a sentiment shared by other conservatives, did feel
the need to put the word *Enlightenment* in scare quotes throughout
his book and to distance himself and fellow conservatives from the
"secular cult of the rationalistic Enlightenment."[12]

Another thing that liberals and conservatives could agree on was
that ideology in any form was an enemy of democracy. "Ideology"
was an epithet they hurled hither and thither to disparage a system
of ideas or a worldview. It was almost never modified by an adjective because its associations were unmistakable. Fascism and
Nazism were ideologies, and Soviet Communism, too, so what
possibly could recommend it? Trilling expressed a view shared by
commentators on the left, right, and center when he suggested in
The Liberal Imagination (1950) that the ease with which parts of
Europe moved from imperialism to fascism to "totalitarian communism" revealed the dangers of a society that put limits on the free
play of the intellect. Illiberal societies become so, he maintained, because they are "bankrupt of ideas": "for in the modern situation it is
just when a movement despairs of having ideas that it turns to force,

which it masks in ideology."[13] Viereck similarly hammered on the dangers of "monolithic, systematized ideology" and a "rigid, ideological definition of the proper role of government."[14] He held that conservativism in America was very different. It was not a program or a dogma but rather "a way of living, of balancing and harmonizing; it is not science but art. Conservatism is the art of listening to the way history grows."[15] By taking up the position that ideology was the absence of critical and careful thinking, both liberal and conservative commentators agreed that democracy was a state of mind.

In addition, liberals and conservatives shared the sentiment of historian Arthur Schlesinger Jr., who claimed in 1949 that the "politics of freedom" could be found only in what he called "the vital center." Schlesinger did not mean the center between Americans left and right.[16] He meant it in a global context, advocating that the postwar United States steer clear of fascism to the right and communism to the left, and keep itself squarely in the "vital center" of the two.

Neither his liberal colleagues nor his conservative detractors disagreed with the sentiment. They simply could not agree where that vital center could be found, and what it would take to make that vital center hold.

Quests for Authenticity

Keeping the American mind open—to new ways of viewing the world, new moral vocabularies, and new aesthetic sensibilities— was in no way easy, given all the very real pressures for conformity during and even after the height of the Red Scare. Midcentury voices of discontent often had to speak in a whisper or in code. But they were, no doubt, audible in popular culture. They could be heard in the aimlessness and antagonism of fictional characters like the disaffected teenager Holden Caulfield in J. D. Salinger's *The Catcher in the Rye* (1951), in the dissatisfaction and estrangement explored in movies like *Blackboard Jungle* (1954) and *Rebel without a Cause* (1955), and in the anti-establishment restlessness and alienation of Allen Ginsberg's and Jack Kerouac's Beat poetry and prose.

The concern about conformity extended into other registers as well, including scholarly studies of American culture and personality. Harvard sociologist David Riesman's *The Lonely Crowd: A Study of the Changing American Character* (1950) showed how the postwar American pressure for uniformity and togetherness was actually producing its opposite. Instead of creating "inner-directed" personality types who are guided by a strong internal conscience, American culture was producing atomized and alienated "other-directed" personalities who run on a "diffuse *anxiety*" and toggle between conformity and anomie, as they chronically seek the affirmation of others in their schools, workplaces, and leisure activities.[17]

Columbia University sociologist C. Wright Mills gave Americans even more reason to worry as he drew attention to the dangers of modern bureaucratic forms of social power and powerlessness. In *White Collar* (1951), he examined middle-class corporation men and business culture, and five years later, in *The Power Elite*, he took his criticism higher up on the social status food chain to the troubling behaviors and worldviews of leaders in business, the military, and politics. He sounded similar alarms in both. Instead of self-possessed thinkers and independent actors, he saw status-seeking "cheerful robots" and technicians, and the "organized irresponsibility" and "mindlessness of the powerful that is the true higher immorality of our time."[18]

While Riesman and Mills provided a sociological interpretation of dislocation and disaffection of the midcentury self, many American readers craved other ways of coming to terms with a vague and ominous sense of "inauthenticity" (to use a keyword of the day) that settled over them after the war. Philosophy and literature were genres in which intellectuals explored the psychic disorientation they were experiencing. The novels and plays of Jean-Paul Sartre, Simone de Beauvoir, and Albert Camus found an eager audience in

America, helping to turn them into intellectual stars and French existentialism into a vogue among young, disillusioned Americans. In fashion magazines and journals of opinion, in newspapers and on television, Americans encountered Sartre with his black spectacles and pipe, de Beauvoir with her long locks rolled into a crown on top of her head, and Camus brooding with a cigarette pursed between his lips. They learned that these thinkers were not part of a school or tradition, but rather practiced a particular style of philosophy and way of being in the world that challenged the alienation of industrial capitalism and class warfare, the brutality of imperialism, the empty promises of modern technology to improve humanity, and the bankruptcy of religious comforts. Readers could discover in their writings that these philosophers were not interested in chasing down cold, barren, abstract ideas, but rather explored the way one experiences his or her existence in the world. The French existentialists were greeted with fascination, though also with some revulsion, by Americans who felt that the horrors of World War II had made a mockery of the Western intellectual tradition and thus sought to reset a notion of the self and the world more in line with their feelings of radical indeterminacy and experiences of aloneness in an anonymous, indifferent world.

African American authors did not need a cataclysmic war to tell them that the world was out of whack or that justice was a chimera, or to feel a deep and abiding sense of cosmic abandonment. This was, for too many of them, part of their lived experience from their early childhoods on. Because these feelings were so familiar to them, Ralph Ellison and Richard Wright were able to render a distinctly American existentialism by drawing on their own haunting experiences with such precision and power. For Ellison, this meant studying the forced invisibility or very public demonization of African Americans. Ellison explained black invisibility in the opening lines of his *Invisible Man* (1950): "I am an invisible man. No, I am not a spook like those who haunted Edgar Allan Poe; nor am I one of your Hollywood-movie ectoplasms. I am a man of

Simone de Beauvoir and Richard Wright and his wife, Ellen, spent time together in New York City in 1947, having begun their warm transatlantic friendship a year earlier in Paris. De Beauvoir had come to travel through the United States and record her observations, as well as her esteem for Wright, in *L'Amérique au jour le jour* (1954). *Nelson Algren papers in the Rare Books and Manuscripts Library of the Ohio State University Libraries*

substance, of flesh and bone, fiber and liquids—and I might even be said to possess a mind. I am invisible, understand, simply because people refuse to see me."[19]

Wright did not need the European existentialists to articulate his ideas. But because what they described so closely aligned with his own understanding, he gravitated to their writings. After growing disillusioned with Marxism in the early 1940s, Wright began reading works by Heidegger and Kierkegaard, which in turn became gateway drugs to other existentialists, both living and dead. Wright spent long hours with the works of Dostoyevsky, Nietzsche, and Husserl; and thanks to tight transatlantic publishing networks, he became good friends with de Beauvoir and Sartre, and he had Albert Camus's help in getting a French edition of *Black Boy* published. Wright even moved permanently to Paris in July 1947, spending the rest of his life in what he called "voluntary exile," because he experienced more freedom in Paris as a foreigner than as a black "native son" in his own America.

But it was Wright's experiences in the United States that gave him a fund of existential dilemmas, hardships, and possibilities to draw from in his fiction and essays. In particular, Wright's novels explore the theme of the individual, who through sheer will and deliberate action tries to create himself without the help of a divine Creator. He explored this isolation and alienation from institutional religion and conventional morality through his protagonists Bigger Thomas in *Native Son* (1940) and Cross Damon in *The Outsider* (1953), and in his own self-portrait in *Black Boy* (1945). Ever the outcast, Damon "had to discover what was good or evil through his own actions which were more exacting than the edicts of any God because it was he alone who had to bear the brunt of their consequences with a sense of absoluteness made intolerable by knowing that this life of his was all he had and would ever have. For him there was no grace of mercy if he failed."[20] There is no mistaking Wright's dark examinations of individual self-making with Horatio Alger's love letters to plucky, rags-to-riches individualism. Wright's novels were instead deeply unsentimental explorations of the ways in which existential freedom can be an achievement, but also a terrible burden.

Religion and the Intellectuals

In the years following World War II, many prominent thinkers came to believe that the atrocities of the twentieth century were the result of modern spiritual disenchantment—not just social dislocations. Over the course of the 1950s and 1960s, a growing number of religious scholars and theologians, psychologists, mythologists, and freelance seekers tried to assess the health of the soul of man under modernity and concluded that it was not good.

And so they found common cause in surveying the world's historical religions, spiritual practices, and philosophical systems for epistemological and moral insights still available to secular moderns. They tried either to dig deeper into human history for truths buried under the ruins of institutional religion or to reach higher to find what Paul Tillich referred to as the "God above God"[21] who did not reside in any one of the world's religions, not even his own Christianity.

These seekers worked within established intellectual venues and created new ones. Some conducted their investigations from the academy—among them émigré historian and philosopher of religion Mircea Eliade at the University of Chicago and mythologist and literary scholar Joseph Campbell at Sarah Lawrence College. Others bridged academic homes and social justice advocacy, such as émigré rabbi and theologian Abraham Joshua Heschel, who divided his time and energies between professorships at Hebrew Union College and Jewish Theological Seminary and civil rights activism. Others helped found new religious institutions and para-academic centers, for example, Howard Thurman, who cofounded the interfaith, interracial Church for the Fellowship of All Peoples in San Francisco in 1944, and Shunryu Suzuki, who founded the San Francisco Zen Center in San Francisco (1962) and later authored the blockbuster *Zen Mind, Beginner's Mind* (1970). Some turned to established presses and magazines, like *Time*, which devoted much of its precious textual real estate—and even lead stories—to religious issues. Others started new publishing ventures, such as the Bollingen Series at Pantheon Books, devoted to translations of Carl Gustav Jung's psychological mysticism and a mix of ancient texts and cutting-edge studies on related themes.

Critical observers of the time could not help but notice the powerful uptick in this interest in religion—if not religiosity—and tried to make sense of it. Not everyone was impressed. The *Partisan Review* called together one of its signature symposia in 1950, this time with W. H. Auden, Dwight Macdonald, Alfred Kazin, Hannah

Arendt, and Marianne Moore to assess the "new turn toward religion among intellectuals." Catholic philosopher Jacques Maritain had to hold back his disdain for the condescension barely contained by the secular editors. "I am not much interested in the new turn toward religion among intellectuals. . . . What is of interest, from the point of view of faith, are the souls, and their orientation toward eternity." Kazin also gently upbraided the editors for somehow suggesting that religious belief and a rigorous intellect could not go hand in hand. He reminded them of Mahatma Gandhi, Christian Socialist Ignazio Silone, and Catholic theologian and labor activist Emmanuel Mounier as examples of men of faith who were also uncompromising intellectuals. Arendt suggested that the return to religion after a "naturalistic" or "positivistic" period is neither unusual nor alarming but just part of historical intellectual cycles. Meanwhile, pragmatist philosopher Sidney Hook, in his typical pugnacious fashion, dusted off an old complaint of his about "the new failure of nerve" of intellectuals gravitating toward "irrationalism" and abandoning the hard-fought achievements in scientific conceptions of open inquiry and verifiability.[22]

The longing for universals among the world's different belief systems fueled these quests. Was there something—anything—that all religious beliefs had in common? British expatriate writer Aldous Huxley, who had moved to Southern California in 1937, began taking a serious interest in Hindu philosophy and meditation. The grandson of the nineteenth-century agnostic scientist Thomas Huxley (known as "Darwin's bulldog"), Aldous inherited his grandfather's iconoclasm, but one that was inflected with a deep curiosity about religion and a strong mystical bent. After writing an introduction to the 1944 translation of *The Bhagavad Gita* by fellow expat British novelist Christopher Isherwood and Swami Prabhavananda of the Vedanta Society of Southern California, Huxley turned to writing his *The Perennial Philosophy* (1945). In it, Huxley focused on what he thought might be the eternally true elements of Hindu, Buddhist, Taoist, Christian, and, to a lesser extent, Islamic and Jewish scripture and history. He characterized the perennial philosophy as those insights that are deeper than the particularities of any one religion and get beneath the creeds, the liturgy, the practices, and the time- and power-bound conceptions of good and evil, and reach to what he believed were the universal truths at their core. For Huxley, any single religious tradition represents truths that have been battered, altered, or hived off by various groups in the messy process of history. However, by lining up different belief systems and philosophies against each other, he hoped that moderns could tap into their shared timeless, much-needed insights.

This longing for perennial spiritual insights helps explain why Jung made significant inroads into American thought at this time. The son of a Lutheran minister who chose modern medicine over the clergy, Jung became the founder of analytic psychology. Following Freud, he believed that human fears and motivations lay in the unconscious mind. Unlike Freud, however, he thought that primal sexual instincts accounted for only some aspects of human civilization and its discontents. For Jung, the religious instinct— what he called the "authentic religious function"—was as powerful.[23] Encoded in man's unconscious mind were more than simply childhood individual experiences but rather the collective experience of all humankind.

To access that collective unconscious, Jung encouraged his American readers to study "archetypes"—"universally present psychic disposition[s]"—that crop up time and again in the world's different religions, philosophies, and myths.[24] To access these archetypes, and to find the universal in the particular, Jung roamed far and wide, bringing yoga, alchemy, tribal religious rituals, and extrasensory perception into the reach of psychology. Jung rejected Freud's focus on sexual drives as the seat of all volition and refused to see religion as a neurosis. Jung's value to midcentury American thought was to make analytic psychology spirituality's handmaiden. Jung thus sought to restore the "psyche" to "psychology," and spiritual questing to modern experience.

Jung's effort to keep modern science from shouting down religion, and "Western" knowledge from overriding the wisdom of the "East," found common cause with a variety of midcentury spiritual seekers eager for the same. It was in 1949 that D. T. Suzuki, after living and teaching in Japan since his departure from the United States in 1908, returned to present at the East-West Philosophers' Conference in Honolulu and to commence his career in postwar American life as an ambassador of Zen Buddhism, influencing psychoanalysts Jung, Erich Fromm, and Karen Horney; Trappist monk and popular Christian writer Thomas Merton; and composer John Cage and Zen poet Gary Snyder, among many others.

In 1962, two Stanford graduates, Michael Murphy and Dick Price, founded the Esalen Institute in Big Sur, California, as a retreat and research center focused on interpenetrations of scientific and religious, Eastern and Western wisdom. Murphy had lived for a year and a half at the Sri Aurobindo Ashram in Pondicherry, India, before meeting Price, who had studied with the Zen philosopher Alan Watts in San Francisco. Lectures and programs combined meditation with gestalt therapy, yoga with humanistic psychology, the occult with evolutionary sciences. In addition, books on the science of spirituality (and vice versa) flooded the 1960s and 1970s marketplace including Fritjof Capra's *The Tao of Physics: An Exploration of the Parallels between Modern Physics and Eastern Mysticism* (1975) and Gary Zukav's *Dancing Wu Li Masters: An Overview of the New Physics* (1979). Capra posed a question driving all of these movements and authors: "Is modern science, with all its sophisticated machinery, merely rediscovering ancient wisdom, known to the Eastern sages for thousands of years?"[25] Their collective answer was yes.

The varieties of intellectual quests of the late 1940s, 1950s, and early 1960s, each in its own way, represented an effort to open American mental and moral horizons. Intellectual seekers thought that if they could properly do so, they might just find that "vital center" they

Time magazine's February 1955 cover story, "The Wise Old Man" (top left), celebrated psychological mystic Carl Jung and his appreciation of the "religious instinct" in human beings. The March 1959 issue (top right) featured theologian Paul Tillich with the headline "Religion. To Be or Not to Be," which played on the title of his 1952 surprise hit, *The Courage to Be*. The April 1959 issue (bottom) informed American readers of his exile from Tibet into northern India and introduced them to the "serenity and peace" of Tibetan Buddhism. *Time, Inc., Meredith Corporation*

were after, whether it be between political stability and individual freedom, a vibrant sense of the "social" and an autonomous self, or the rigors of science and the consolations of religions. Seekers for meaning may not have noticed the trickle of "exhaustion" theories calling into question their efforts to find universalizing doctrines. That is likely because the first of them, Daniel Bell's *The End of Ideology: On the Exhaustion of Political Ideas in the Fifties* (1960), announcing the bankruptcy of revolutionary worldviews and chiliastic dreams, probably did come about a decade too soon, given that the 1960s was a decade of passionate social and political doctrines of all sorts. But the timing for novelist John Barth's warning about "the literature of exhaustion" in a lecture he gave at the University of Virginia in 1967 was just about right. He observed a "used-upness" of all heretofore available literary forms and suggested that "ultimacies" in literature were being replaced by a "labyrinth" of endless choices, innumerable directions, but also many, many dead ends. And this is what the postmodern era, just then slowly getting its start, was about to bring.[26]

Chapter 8

Against Universalism: 1962–90s

Few decades in American history are as fabled as the 1960s. They were years of great hope as activists, lawyers, and governmental officials translated American liberal ideas into civil rights laws and Great Society social reforms. They were also years of dashed dreams as the full benefit of those liberal achievements was undercut by the Vietnam War, which drained resources from American cities to ramp up the war effort in Vietnamese provincial towns, remote villages, and jungles. The military campaigns may have taken place halfway around the world, but the battlefronts extended into American homes, dividing loyalties between parents and their children, and into city streets as angry protesters clashed with riot police. It was a decade in which a number of visionary and inspiring political leaders, including Martin Luther King Jr., John F. Kennedy, Malcolm X, and Robert Kennedy, rallied millions to their cause. But it was also the decade in which their lives—and much of the hope they inspired—were cut short by assassins' bullets.

If "the sixties" evoke images of a decade in which high hopes and daring dreams spiraled into protest and violence, they are also remembered as a period in which these political and social conflicts generated emancipatory ideas of all kinds. The standard historical narrative tells how these contestations produced visions, some realized and others deferred, of the liberation of blacks from white oppression, women from male dominance, gay pride from homophobia, Afros from straightened hair, breasts from bras, the environment from pesticides and overdevelopment, and the younger generation's life paths from the older generation's best-laid plans.

Though the sixties were, no doubt, a period of intense cultural ferment, the traditional explanation that the political and social tumult of the period produced radical ideas reverses cause and effect by viewing American politics and society as the conditions producing radical ideas, rather than understanding how earlier ideas helped create those very conditions. So many of the radical ideas that convulsed the period were produced early in the decade (before the Big Bang version of the period typically commences), and these are the revolutionary claims that went on to realign American intellectual life for the remainder of the century. To be sure, parsing cause from effect is one of the most difficult challenges in understanding historical change. But the case of "the sixties" suggests that ideas have been historical stimuli, not merely symptoms. Another way to put this is that "the sixties"—and the dramatic decades that followed—started in *ideas*.

1962 or Thereabouts

The year 1962 does not announce itself as a significant turning point in history. It does not have the convenient clarity to mark a beginning like 1607, when the first English colonists arrived in America, or 1776 with the Declaration of Independence. Nor is it an 1848, a year when the Mexican American War ended; the California gold rush began; the quest for women's rights rocked Seneca Falls, New York; and liberal revolutions shook Europe. The year 1962 is not even closely associated with a traumatic event like 1929, when the American stock market crashed so spectacularly that its devastating ripple effects were felt around the world.

The year 1962 does not rival these other years as exceptionally momentous in American political and social history. As with any calendar year in history, some important events did take place. It was the year of the Cuban Missile Crisis, John Glenn's orbit around Earth, and Jackie Robinson's election to the Baseball Hall of Fame (the first for an African American). It was also the year when Cesar Chavez founded the United Farm Workers; Kmart opened its first store in Garden City, Michigan; and the animated series about a futurist family, *The Jetsons*, premiered on television. These are not insignificant milestones. But on the whole, 1962 is not one of those years packed with larger social and political significance.

But from the vantage point of American intellectual history, 1962 (or thereabouts) is crowded with major publications and events that realigned the paths of American thought and culture that lead up to today's America. It is the year when Rachel Carson published her exposé *Silent Spring*, revealing the detrimental effects of synthetic pesticides and launching the modern environmental movement. It is the year when Michael Harrington's *The Other America*, a ground-breaking study of poverty in America, became a surprise bestseller that shaped the Great Society programs and debates about the "culture of poverty" for decades to come. It is the year when Ken Kesey's *One Flew over the Cuckoo's Nest* hit on the theme of how those marked "insane" prove to be less sick than the society that labels them as such, foreshadowing a mode of biting cultural criticism in the dog days of the Vietnam War. And it is the year when Andy Warhol first exhibited his thirty-two *Campbell's Soup Cans* canvases, stacked one on top of the other and packed side by side, mimicking all the stately beauty and refinement of a grocery store shelf.

What is remarkable about the intellectual works of 1962 or thereabouts is not only the perspicacity with which they addressed pressing issues but also the ways in which they foreshadowed, and even influenced, the central preoccupations in American thought for decades to come. For example, Marshall McLuhan's *The Gutenberg Galaxy: The Making of Typographic Man*, which explores how communication technologies fundamentally transformed the human beings who used them, helped establish the fields of communication and media studies by showing how, as he later put it, "the medium is the message."[1] "Language is metaphor in the sense that it not only stores but translates experience from one mode into another," McLuhan wrote. "The principle of exchange and translation, or metaphor, is in our rational power to translate all of our senses into one another. This we do every instant of our lives. But the price we pay . . . is that these massive *extensions* of sense constitute *closed* systems."[2] McLuhan's warning about the flattening tendencies of mass society broke open the discursive space for Herbert Marcuse's *One Dimensional Man: Studies in the Ideology of Advanced Industrial Society* (1964), while his critique of the alienating effects of technology would help set the terms for Robert Pirsig's *Zen and the Art of Motorcycle Maintenance* (1974). The sentiments expressed in *The Gutenberg Galaxy* would help to make the related logic of deconstruction, and with it Jacques Derrida's proclamation that "there is nothing outside the text" a decade later seem a little less implausible.[3]

It may be hard to imagine that the leftist Students for a Democratic Society's (SDS) Port Huron Statement and the staunchly libertarian economist Milton Friedman's *Capitalism and Freedom* came out in the same year, but it shows how concerns about the effects and possibilities of postwar American prosperity captured the attention of critical observers in the early 1960s. In June 1962, fifty-nine members of the SDS, inspired by the civil rights movement and focused similarly on issues of racial equality, economic justice, and peace, came together at a labor union resort in Michigan to draft a manifesto for their movement. In it, they laid out the contours of "participatory democracy"—"the art of collectively creating an acceptable pattern of social relations."[4]

These young leftists could not have used words more anathema to University of Chicago economics professor Milton Friedman's ideal vision of a democratic society if they had tried. For Friedman, the most prominent face of the "Chicago School" of economics and its most vigorous critic of Keynesian (or state-interventionist) economics, the best thing a democratic government could do was to get out of its citizens' way. Translating his technical expertise into accessible and engaging prose for a general audience, Friedman's wildly popular *Capitalism and Freedom* maintained that governmental regulations were strangling freedom not just out of the market but out of American political life as well. He asserted that "the invisible hand has been more potent for progress than the visible hand for retrogression."[5] The vision of progress he laid out in rather jaunty, upbeat prose included abolishing the minimum wage, the licensing of doctors, and fair employment laws, as well as advocating for vouchers for public schools. While the Port Huron Statement helped re-establish a Progressive-era style of yoking cultural and political criticism to enable a more holistic way of talking about a democratic society, *Capitalism and Freedom* helped exalt "free choice" and "the market" as indisputable moral goods. An odd couple if there ever was one, they showed how the most persuasive claims for a welfare state and the most alluring arguments for laissez-faire principles simultaneously secured the prominent place they have in Americans' notions about the economy today.

Less than a year later, two transformative texts would add to this lineup, breaking apart conventional ideas of the proper social "place" for women and people of color while helping to strengthen their respective liberation movements: Betty Friedan's *The Feminine Mystique* and Martin Luther King Jr.'s "Letter from Birmingham Jail". Both are a form of prison writing—Friedan from the gilded cage of her suburban home, and King from an Alabama jail cell, where he was held in solitary confinement for violating a court injunction against public protests.

Friedan was a wife, the mother of three, and a labor activist turned journalist for women's magazines before coming to terms with the fact that the magazines she wrote for contributed to white, middle-class women's "problem that has no name." She argued that the "comfortable concentration camp" of the midcentury cult of motherhood and femininity kept women out of the workforce, beholden to their husbands, and tethered to diaper bags, grocery shopping carts, and PTA meetings.[6] Friedan drew on de Beauvoir's *Second Sex* (1949) in lamenting that women still regarded men as the measure of what it is to be human while taking Freudian analysis to task for perpetuating myths about women's sexuality that gave scientific respectability to outmoded gender ideals. She invoked Mary Wollstonecraft, Angelina Grimké, Elizabeth Cady Stanton, and Margaret Fuller as the first wave of feminist striving, thereby helping her launch what would come to be known as second-wave feminism.

King wrote his letter in response to a "Call for Unity" issued by eight white fellow clergymen, who encouraged African Americans to abandon their protests and leave it to the courts to work out the terms of their fate as American citizens. His audience, however, was broader than that. In his letter, he sought to grab moderate whites by their consciences and shake them free of their muddled arguments for incrementalism. King wanted to redirect their concern from the effects of protests to the myriad causes for them. The letter recognized sympathetic whites' desire for racial equality while chastising their timidity to make the time *now* to achieve it. "We have waited for more than 340 years for our constitutional and God-given rights," King wrote before cataloging the abuses visited upon African Americans on a daily basis and emphasizing that only just laws, not unjust ones, demanded assent: "We should never forget that everything Adolf Hitler did in Germany was 'legal' and everything the Hungarian freedom fighters did in Hungary was 'illegal.'" He presented a vigorous case for direct nonviolent action suffused with love as a necessary and legitimate "force" to negotiate a future for African Americans. And he reminded his readers of the obvious: "Freedom is never voluntarily given by the oppressor; it must be demanded by the oppressed."[7]

Though exploring different struggles and addressing themselves to different audiences, Friedan's and King's texts did similar intellectual work in the early 1960s. They provided women and African Americans, respectively, with a trenchant critique of contemporary thought, customs, and law, while offering them, in turn, a vision of equality, justice, and human flourishing.

There is one more crucial text of this moment that was neither an overnight bestseller like Friedan's book nor widely discussed in the popular press like King's letter. Nevertheless, it had subtle but penetrating effects that would sneak up on the natural sciences, the human sciences, and ethical thought in the late twentieth century. Thomas Kuhn's *The Structure of Scientific Revolutions* (1962) fundamentally challenged long-standing notions of science as a purely objective enterprise. The central idea of the book is that scientific investigation typically takes place in "normal" periods of conventional practice, shared values, and intellectual consensus—what Kuhn called a "paradigm." But a crisis emerges when a paradigm's tools and language are not able to deal effectively with evidentiary "anomalies." In Kuhn's account, scientific revolutions occur when a rival paradigm comes forth to successfully account for the anomaly, thereby superseding the old one.

This could all seem perfectly uncontroversial but for the fact that, according to Kuhn, scientific knowledge from the earlier paradigm is "incommensurable" with that of the latter paradigm. This meant, in effect, that there is no common measure for different scientific paradigms, no airtight way for a paradigm to apprehend an absolute or external "reality" independent of its means of apprehension, and no clear progress in the move from one paradigm to another.

The shocking and controversial implications of Kuhn's argument radiated out into virtually all fields of scientific and humanistic inquiry. If science does not provide objective measures that transcend all paradigms, how can we decide between contradictory claims of truth if they are wholly relative to one's particular paradigmatic point of view? Does "incommensurability" mean that reason, rational inquiry, and indisputable evidence are not actually the ways we adjudicate different claims of truth? If science is the study of an external reality by means of social constructs, does that mean that all scientific knowledge is merely a social construct too? *Structure* became one of the most cited academic texts of the second half of the century, primarily because the answers to these questions had such high stakes in virtually every domain of scholarly inquiry. By dismantling science as a domain of absolute truth, *Structure* sparked an intellectual revolution of its own, accrediting antifoundationalist ideas that would become the opening salvo of late twentieth-century American postmodernism.

The American Discovery of Postmodernism

Kuhn never identified himself as a postmodernist, and, indeed, it was quite some time before American thinkers would claim him to be one. This was so because, for much of the late 1960s and 1970s, postmodernism was seen as a French import.

In the late 1960s, a growing number of (mostly) French philosophers began to advance a style of thought that would come to be known as postmodernism (and its variants poststructuralism and deconstruction) while launching their careers as celebrities in American academic literary circles. Some, like Gilles Deleuze, Pierre Klossowski, and Luce Irigaray, came only periodically to participate in a conference, give a lecture, or promote an English translation of one of their books. Others, such as Paul de Man, Jacques Derrida, Jean-François Lyotard, and Michel Foucault, came to hold professorships or make extended stays at American universities, thus securing a more direct and sustained impact on their American readers. The mystique of their ideas, the charisma of their personas, and the dramas and controversies that followed them and their theories made it seem to many observers that these European intellectual superstars were bringing a radically new—and even reckless—mode of anti-universalist thinking to America, and with it a host of moral and epistemological messes for Americans to clean up after them.

Though the term *postmodernism* first gained traction in intellectual discourses as a way to characterize dramatic changes in 1960s aesthetics, it quickly became associated with an emerging intellectual style in philosophy, literary theory, and social criticism. A way of thinking that insists that the intellectual center of all claims to knowledge does not hold, postmodernism is thus quite difficult to characterize. There are, nevertheless, shared assumptions, commitments, and methods that help identify it. Postmodernism is skeptical of all binary oppositions, rejecting the distinction between "objectivity" and "subjectivity" most vociferously. Once "objectivity" is out, so too is the notion that one's perception links up to an absolute reality. Many postmodern theorists thus pushed for a McLuhan-like approach to language by demonstrating how language constructs reality rather than simply representing it transparently. They also challenged beliefs or practices claimed to be rooted in nature, arguing that all truths are shaped by human will, desire, and habits. They gave a new name for an old Jamesian way of thinking, calling this "anti-essentialism" where William James described it as a recognition that "the trail of the human serpent is . . . over everything." In addition, they took umbrage at the universalist assumptions of something they referred to as "the Enlightenment Project," which was also a new formulation at this time. Jean-François Lyotard helped to give all these various strains of radical skepticism some coherence in *The Postmodern Condition: A Report on Knowledge* (1979) when he characterized their common stance as "incredulity toward metanarratives."[8]

The philosopher and psychiatrist Michel Foucault was the thinker who made the most damning criticisms of the Enlightenment project. Of all the postmodernists, he concerned himself most explicitly, and most forcefully, with questions about "power" once divine and even natural bases for it are called into question. How are intellectual, psychological, and social forms of power, authority, and domination expressed, and where do they come from? How are they justified and maintained? To answer these questions, Foucault developed

Rejecting what he saw as the stale formalism of modernist architecture, architect Frank Gehry helped usher in a postmodern aesthetic, which rejected rectilinear shapes and jettisoned a visual center. "Postmodernism" first gained traction in American thought through its association with a new aesthetic in architecture before it was enlisted to describe movements in philosophy and literature. *Weisman Art Museum (completed 1993), University of Minnesota; Justin Ladia/Flickr*

what he called "archaeological" and "genealogical" approaches to the study of social configurations of power as they manifest themselves in worldviews, institutions, and cultural practices. In *Discipline and Punish* (1975), Foucault extended his investigation of the genealogy of moral codes by looking into the development of modern, more "humane" and "enlightened" approaches to punishing social deviants. These reforms aimed, in his words, "to punish less, but to punish better."[9] Foucault extended his study of prisons to understand how new modes of policing, control, surveillance, and reform extended into modern factories, hospitals, schools, and the military, and, in doing so, created a modern system of disciplinary power. Foucault thus helped popularize, like Ken Kesey before him, a skepticism about the "helping professions" and seemingly benign forms of social education and control, asserting that modern notions of health and well-being were themselves quite sick.

Had so many American academics in the humanities in the 1970s, 1980s, and 1990s not found the postmodernists' ideas about the contingency of truth, the manipulations of language, and the ambiguity of moral regimes so persuasive, the vogue of French theorists might have just been another fleeting intellectual fashion. But because a vocal minority of academics began working with postmodern ideas and interpretive strategies, even turning their spokespeople into adjectives for this way of thinking ("Foucauldian," "Derridean"), worried observers sounded the alarm that a "foreign invasion" was infecting the academy and, by extension, the tender minds of impressionable students.

University of Chicago classics professor Allan Bloom did the most to popularize the intellectual transformations of the 1970s and 1980s as a foreign invasion, and with his clever and persuasive histrionics turned himself into an equally high-wattage intellectual superstar until his death in 1992. In his runaway bestseller *The Closing of the American Mind: How Higher Education Has Failed Democracy and Impoverished the Souls of Today's Students*, Bloom cautioned that these rampant antifoundational ideas had foreign pedigrees. However, in his retelling they stemmed not from postwar French thought but rather from late nineteenth-century German philosophy, in particular Nietzsche's moral relativism. According to Bloom, when Americans went for "no fault divorces," "conflict resolution," and "political correctness" instead of adjudicating the truth, they were simply putting into practice the nonsense being taught in the college classroom. He was not belittling Nietzsche and the European thinkers who followed him. He was simply arguing that Americans had become "Philistines" after the convulsions of the 1960s, and by becoming too distrustful of moral authority they were deploying a dumbed-down "value relativism" from Europe. "All awareness of foreignness disappears," Bloom repined. Little did college students and their baby boomer professors and parents realize that these dark assaults on moral universalism had no place "on enchanted American ground."[10]

Though American practitioners of antifoundationalism certainly did not agree with Bloom's diagnosis, many would have assumed he was right in his assessment that ideas trafficking under the rubric of "postmodernism" had a foreign provenance. Indeed, for some, that was their appeal. Thus, when a historian would later cite American postmodernism as an "exemplary adventure in intellectual dissemination," he made a claim many assumed to be true.[11] What is missing in this account (as only a very few astute observers at the time noticed) is that these varieties of European antifoundationalism were making such big strides in late twentieth-century American life primarily because they were tapping into intellectual habits and commitments long present in American thought.

But just two years after the publication of Bloom's jeremiad, a young Princeton University professor of religion named Cornel West sought to set the record straight. With his *American Evasion of Philosophy: A Genealogy of Pragmatism*, West argued that the "evasion of epistemology-centered philosophy" was something bequeathed to late twentieth-century Americans by their own "indigenous" Emerson. He had no objection to calling this "postmodernism," so long as it was clear to his American readers that this philosophy was their own native tradition of pragmatism coming back dressed in a new linguistic garb. Some other neo-pragmatists, a group of thinkers intent on refocusing attention on the writings of the founders of American pragmatism, were uncomfortable with this comparison. For West, "American pragmatism is less a philosophical tradition putting forward solutions to perennial problems in the Western philosophical conversation . . . and more a continuous cultural commentary or set of interpretations that attempt to explain America to itself at a particular historical moment." It was a way of thinking particularly well fitted to an American landscape with a "confused populace caught in the whirlwinds of societal crisis, the cross fires of ideological polemics, and the storms of class, racial, and gender conflicts."[12] Emerson understood this. So too did James and Dewey after him. And so too were Americans again, at the end of the century, welcoming an intellectual "evasiveness" (West's term for the move away from epistemological foundations and toward situational, contextual problem solving). As West understood it, the vogue of postmodernism was nothing more than Americans recognizing their own rejected thoughts coming back to them with a certain alienated majesty.

Identity Politics and the Culture Wars

If Bloom fired the first shot of the "culture wars" with his *Closing of the American Mind*, he soon got reinforcement from high-profile pundits and politicians, who treated these postmodern endorsements of intellectual fragmentation and subversion with disdain. Most were variations on a theme charging that the assaults on universals were creating a pernicious gospel of "multiculturalism" in the academy, which was just another means to relativistic ends. Historian Arthur M. Schlesinger Jr. sounded the alarm with his 1991 *The Disuniting of America: Reflections on a Multicultural Society*. He argued that academics had degenerated into ethnic activists and that advocates were proselytizing to students a way of thinking about America that "belittles *unum* and glorifies *pluribus*."[13]

Throughout much of the 1970s and early 1980s, one fault line contributing to a sense of a disunited state of America was one long familiar to observers: individualism. There is no period in American history when thinkers have not wrestled with the appropriate balance of power between self-interest and social obligation (think back to republicanism, transcendentalism, and progressivism). But it was at this time that a number of writers offered up new ways of conceptualizing America's cultural premium on an atomistic, even antisocial, conception of the self. In a 1976 *New York* magazine article, "The 'Me' Decade and the Third Great Awakening," satirist Tom Wolfe ridiculed what he saw as the profligacy and excesses of the burgeoning self-help movement of the period: "The old alchemical dream was changing base metals into gold. The new alchemical dream is: changing one's personality—remaking, remodeling, elevating, and polishing one's very *self*... and observing, studying, and doting on it. (Me!)."[14]

The historian and cultural critic Christopher Lasch chimed in with an even more devastating critique, *The Culture of Narcissism: American Life in an Age of Diminishing Expectations* (1979). Lasch turned the word *narcissism*—which up until then was a very specific clinical term of Freud's to diagnose a pathology in an individual—into a way of characterizing the American personality. The narcissist, Lasch insisted, was not someone puffed up on her or his own self-worth. Rather, the narcissist had a frail ego, was choked with rage and self-loathing, and therefore turned to others for her or his insatiable need for love and confirmation. For Lasch, a culture of narcissists has no concept of—or longing for—larger structures of meaning and obligation once provided by religious and even political commitments. Lasch's alarm reached the ears of President Jimmy Carter, who invited him to the White House, and Carter later drew on his ideas as he formulated his "crisis of confidence" speech addressing the energy crisis of 1979. Carter warned that the problem facing Americans was not a shortage of gas but a shortage of public spiritedness: a "path that leads to fragmentation and self-interest. Down that road lies a mistaken idea of freedom."[15]

Schlesinger, however, was less concerned about atomistic individualism breaking up public spiritedness and more upset by the ethnic, racial, and other group identity rifts running through academic departments on university campuses. In 1968, the first black studies and Chicano studies programs were founded. In 1970 came the first women's studies and Native American studies programs. Within a few years, these programs had multiplied exponentially across the country. All of them were born of liberation struggles—black studies from the Black Power movement, women's studies from radical feminism, and so on. The courses of study, like the political movements they grew out of, were explicitly and unapologetically based on group identity. For American students and their professors who recognized themselves as members of oppressed groups, the purpose of identity-based curricula was to demand recognition in relevant fields of study and on the college campus. "Our foremost plight is our transparency," wrote Sioux lawyer and activist Vine Deloria Jr. in *Custer Died for Your Sins: An Indian Manifesto* (1969). "The more we try to be ourselves the more we are forced to defend what we have never been.... To be an Indian in modern American society is in a very real sense to be unreal and ahistorical."[16] The various "studies" programs thus sought to reverse this long-standing erasure from the historical record of American knowledge production, to reclaim the lost history and knowledge of their group, and to use organic epistemologies to enable victims of oppression to challenge white, male, heterosexual standards and truth claims.

Not long after these different "studies" programs began making a significant impact on college curricula and campuses, the intellectual effects of postmodernism were radiating out in such a way as to call them into question. If there was a governing logic to American thought in the 1980s, it was to add fault lines to fault lines. It first came in the form of theorists complicating such categories of racial and ethnic identity by showing their "intersectionality" with class, gender, sexual orientation, religion, and region. The poet Audre Lorde provides a glimpse into why some insisted that categories of identity and belonging needed to be rethought. "As a forty-nine-year-old Black lesbian feminist socialist mother of two, including one boy, and a member of an interracial couple, I usually find myself a part of some group defined as other, deviant, inferior, or just plain wrong."[17] It was not long after these identitarian claims posed serious challenges to conventional academic disciplines and practices that postmodernism applied pressure to their assumptions by stressing that they were built on the crumbling foundations of essentialism. Postmodernism thus encouraged scholars specializing in race, ethnicity, and gender to rethink the integrity and stability of their most basic terms of self-description.

Judith Butler, professor of comparative literature and rhetoric at the University of California at Berkeley, was one of the most powerful theorists, and certainly the most popular, to question the assumptions and categorical thinking of fellow feminists. In her groundbreaking book *Gender Trouble: Feminism and the Subversion of Identity* (1990), Butler called into question the "foundationalist fictions" of the sex/gender divide, which viewed sex as something rooted in biology, and gender as constructed by culture. Both, in her view, were neither products of nature nor of necessity but rather the byproducts of a long heteronormative history, with language—and the ability to name—a site of power. But she went further than that to argue that even the category of "woman" itself is a fiction and a "site of contested meanings" produced by a culture invested in regulating the "subjects" created by those fictions. Butler employed Nietzsche's and Foucault's genealogical method of unraveling the historical modes of domination and power knotted up in late twentieth century categories of thought. Our language for gender is merely the performance of outmoded regulatory regimes. Butler, with a flair for difficult phrasing that seemed both unnecessarily inelegant and yet somehow oracular, pronounced: "there is no gender identity behind the expressions of gender; . . . identity is performatively constituted by the very 'expressions' that are said to be its results."[18]

The concept of "race" came under similar scrutiny in the 1980s and 1990s, thereby challenging the most basic assumptions of black and ethnic liberation campaigns. These movements aimed to release "people of color" (itself an invented category, which surged in popularity in this period) from the constraints of prejudice filtered into the arena of language, where even the most basic categories of racial and ethnic thought ("black," "Hispanic," and "race" itself) were thrown into question. Philosopher and professor of Afro-American

American artist Barbara Kruger's *Untitled (You Are Not Yourself)* (1981) visually rendered the postmodern death of the subject, while speaking to various forms of female oppression—both externally imposed and internally safeguarded. Kruger became best known for her black-and-white photographs with staccato texts meant to unsettle the viewer's assumptions about herself, and about American politics and culture. *Mary Boone Galleries*

studies at Harvard Kwame Anthony Appiah argued that the latest research challenging the biological basis of contemporary ideas about
race demanded the rethinking of racial categories altogether. In his
magisterial study *In My Father's House: Africa in the Philosophy of
Culture* (1992), he interrogated the "metaphysical or mythical unity"
to conceptions of "Africa" in Pan-Africanism, African and African
American studies, and Western philosophy more broadly, while
trying to underscore "the illusions of race." "In a sense," observed
Appiah, "trying to classify people into a few races is like trying to
classify books in a library: you may use a single property—size,
say—but you will get a useless classification. . . . No one—not even
the most compulsive librarian!—thinks that book classifications reflect deep facts about books. . . . And nobody thinks that a library
classification can settle which books we should value."[19]

At the same time, discussions of a "postracial" and "postethnic"
America called into question not just the integrity but also the use-
fulness of racial and ethnic essentialism. Having long been a student
of historical notions of American cosmopolitanism, the University of
California–Berkeley intellectual historian David Hollinger updated
Randolph Bourne's criticism of the pluralistic schema of a "melting
pot" multiculturalism by arguing instead for fluid notions of identity,
belonging, and solidarity more in line with late twentieth-century
American realities. "Fewer and fewer Americans believe in biological reality of races," Hollinger observed, "but they are remarkably
willing to live with an officially sanctioned system of demographic
classification [in the census] that replicates precisely the crude, col-
loquial categories, black, yellow, white, red, and brown."[20]

As Appiah and Hollinger tried to imagine new forms of cosmopolitan affiliation without essentials, they were not naïve about the
consequences of anti-essentialist ideas for American minorities'
experiences. Appiah understood that jettisoning "the biological
category of the Negro" should "leave nothing for racists to have an
attitude toward," but they would find a way.[21] Indeed, works like
Heritage Foundation commentator Dinesh D'Souza's *The End*

of Racism (1995) demonstrated how readily conservative critics moved in to adopt a similar challenge to the biological basis of race—not to overcome racism, but to show that black people's cultural deficiencies and their white liberal enablers were to blame. Accepting that race had no biological basis, but not the cultural relativism that could accompany such an acknowledgment, D'Souza lamented that "relativism has now imprisoned liberals in an iron cage that prevents them from acknowledging black pathology."[22] Unsurprisingly, culture war conservatives found D'Souza's bold argument persuasive and hoped more claims of this sort would help bring an end to the politics of racial grievance and government interventions on behalf of minorities. But African American commentators, who like D'Souza utilized anti-essentialism's challenge to racial categories, strenuously disagreed that the end of race in any way meant the end of racism. As comedian Chris Rock put it in one of his stand-up routines in the late 1990s: "There ain't a white man in this room who'd change places with me. None of ya! And I'm rich!"[23]

Challenging the essentialist assumptions of race was particularly fraught for black intellectuals, because they sought affective bonds deeper and more absolute than the shared experience of systematic oppression to define themselves. As a result, the most demanding analyses of racial and ethnic anti-essentialism came not from conservative culture warriors, but rather from the very minorities intended to benefit from it. One of the most chastening observations came from the black feminist philosopher bell hooks, who warily observed: "We should indeed [be] suspicious of postmodern critiques of the 'subject' when they surface at a historical moment when many subjugated people feel themselves coming to voice for the first time." Though hooks felt herself to be "on the outside of the discourse [of 'white male intellectuals and/or academic elites'] looking in," she nevertheless agreed with Appiah that if "such a critique [of essentialism] allows us to affirm multiple black identities, varied black experience," and challenge "colonial imperialist paradigms of black identity," which she felt worked to "reinforce and sustain white supremacy," then the potential payoffs for postmodernism might be worth the risk of forging "blackness" without absolutes.[24]

Wherever late twentieth-century antifoundationalist thinkers found a category of analysis, a concept, or a truth claiming to be absolute, they called it out as an artifact of human quests for power as opposed to a window onto reality. Their efforts aroused their interlocutors' and readers' enthusiasm, gratitude, concern, and outrage, as well as plenty of ridicule, but rarely indifference. But while the challenges to universalism generated passionate responses to their various critiques, nowhere were the reactions as volatile and the stakes as high as when its logic rippled out to theories about civil and, most especially, human rights.

Only the most perspicuous observers noticed the apparent inconsonance of what Rice University historian Thomas Haskell in 1987 referred to as "The Curious Persistence of Rights Talk in the 'Age of Interpretation.'"[25] Soon after, prominent scholars and activists engaged in symposia and attended conferences about whether it was possible to be against universalism and for human rights. They wanted to figure out: Should a truly incredulous "incredulity toward metanarratives" recuse itself when it brushes up against universalist notions with vital and demonstrable benefits for life in a civil society such as human rights? Is there any way for antifoundationalism and rights discourse to find common ground or negotiate a peace agreement?

In 1992, Amnesty International held its first Oxford Amnesty Lecture Series to address this question. As the organization put it in a letter of invitation to speakers, including literary theorists Barbara Johnson, Edward Said, Wayne Booth, and Terry Eagleton: "Our lecturers are being asked to consider the consequences of the deconstruction of the self for the liberal tradition. Does the self as construed by the liberal tradition still exist? If not, whose human rights are we defending?"[26] That antifoundationalism could have enough intellectual firepower to take down rights struck its critics as a sign that the American mind not only had closed but also was sealed shut against any hope of reason and sobriety. That antifoundationalism could have enough intellectual firepower to take down rights struck its theorists and defenders as one of the most pressing issues they needed to reckon with. The problems posed by antifoundationalism were then—and remain today— varied and complex. But while the discourse for so many felt so new and so disorienting, it grew out of intellectual concerns and habits of thinking long familiar in American intellectual life. The debates that ensued were yet a new iteration of the persistent ques- tion of how to build bridges over abysses in moral viewpoints, to create common ground when there are no shared moral grounds to find. This is the question American observers would ask as they found themselves in an age of globalization.

Epilogue: Rethinking America in

an Age of Globalization; or,

The Conversation Continues

When historians use the word *consensus* to describe moral sentiments in a particular period, it is easy to think that they mean *unanimity*. But that is almost never the case. What they mean by *consensus*, rather, is that there are moments in American life when clearly identifiable concerns command the attention of a variety of Americans all along the social and political spectrum. At the turn of the twenty-first century, "globalization" became one of these consensus issues as Americans appreciated the degree to which their lives were affected by large-scale, transnational, and geopolitical developments. In many respects *globalization* was a new term for familiar concerns in American thought. It was yet another iteration of the meaning of America not as a given fact but as a question to answer.

In addition to the popular press, which regularly ran features on the growing interconnectivity of national economies and political orders, a virtual industry of books on the subject flooded the marketplace. Benjamin Barber's *Jihad vs. McWorld: How Globalism and Tribalism Are Reshaping the World* (1995), Samuel Huntington's *The Clash of Civilizations and the Remaking of the World Order* (1996), Noam Chomsky's *Profit over People: Neoliberalism and Global Order* (1999), and Anthony Giddens's *Runaway World: How Globalization Is Reshaping Our*

Lives (1999) were among the major books on globalization and its discontents. College campuses also became disseminators of ideas and hubs for debate about what it meant to be both an American citizen and a citizen of the world. Campaigns in the 1980s for universities to divest from South Africa gave way to student boycotts of campus paraphernalia produced in Asian sweatshops, and to the omnipresent dorm room iconography of Amnesty International's candle wrapped in barbed wire.

The perils and possibilities of globalization and its implications for American life became a shared focus of intense debate. What vexed so many thinkers was how globalization seemed to intensify nationalism around the world instead of breaking it down. They looked historically, economically, and sociologically at the forces that contributed to a national belonging, while assessing the need for twenty-first-century Americans to feel bonds of affiliation, obligation, and reciprocity beyond the nation. "Globalization" was thus a new framework and scale for long-standing and familiar ways of thinking about the boundaries of moral communities, and how or if to refashion identities in the face of a diverse world and uncertain future.

Benedict Anderson's *Imagined Communities: Reflections on the Origins and Spread of Nationalism* (1983) emerged as one of the foremost books shaping conversations about nationalism in the late twentieth-century United States. Though primarily a scholar of Southeast Asia, Anderson looked at various parts of the globe to consider the origins and integrative processes of a felt "deep, horizontal comradeship" with others far and wide. The questions he asked originated in his extended study of Indonesia, a patchwork of people with an intense sense of nationalism, but extended to all pluralistic nations. How do people from different ethnic and linguistic groups come to feel part of something larger called "the nation"? Under what circumstances does that larger national community hold together or fall apart? How could something so abstract as "the nation" inspire such love and devotion, making its subjects willing to kill and die for it? He answered by demonstrating how economic changes coupled with a revolution in communication (popularized by Marshall McLuhan two decades before) helped produce what he referred to as "print-capitalism," which disseminated a sense of commonality or what he called an "imagined community."[1] Anderson's idea of "imagined communities" became one of the most important concepts of twentieth-century political theory around the globe.

If national community was something people "imagined," then wasn't it subject to the very limits of those imaginers' cognitive and moral maps? Though imagining communities could be a positive force, could it not also be a negative one, by imagining some people out of the national community? These questions concerned many observers of this period. The same year that Anderson's study appeared, the Mexican American author Richard Rodriguez published his autobiography, *Hunger of Memory*, to explore what it was like for him, as a dark-skinned, bilingual child of immigrants, to try to become part of the American community. Almost seven decades after Randolph Bourne pushed for a "trans-national America," his ideal still proved to be a distant dream for too many immigrants and their children.

It was also at this time that a growing number of predominantly male gay activists across the country tried unsuccessfully to get the federal government and their fellow citizens to consider homosexuals part of the American imagined community. Their most urgent issue was getting Americans to commit resources to fighting the AIDS epidemic, which was turning their community into what one observer at the time described as a "killing field."[2] But instead of help, they were greeted with ferocious homophobia, and instead of being treated as members of the American community, they were forced to perform do-it-yourself organizing and volunteering to save whatever lives they could.

Meanwhile, at the outermost edges of the American imagination, record numbers of people became homeless, some of whom were featured in Mike Davis's dystopian *City of Quartz: Excavating the Future in Los Angeles* (1990). Davis's postmodern Los Angeles exhibited glitz and grotesqueness in equal measure, as its wealthy inhabitants built private fortresses to protect their luxurious lifestyles from the urban poor. In disturbing detail, Davis showed how, in creating an imagined community of happy, white, rich Los Angelinos, urban planners had so fetishized private privilege that they drafted public spaces out of the American urban imaginary.

As American observers continued to wonder about the "us" and "them" and the "me" versus "we," it was rare for them to turn to professional philosophers in the academy to help them answer their questions. Since midcentury, academic philosophy had increasingly come to focus its attention on logic and linguistic analysis. Professional philosophers had by and large dispensed with questions about ethics, aesthetics, and, most especially, the "meaning of life." This type of inquiry seemed fuzzy, sentimental, and unable to stand up to the rigors of scientific analysis. It was in this atmosphere of logical analysis free of varieties of intellectual fuzziness that Richard Rorty, arguably the most important and influential American philosopher of the second half of the century, got his start. He and his fellow philosophical analysts would never have addressed issues of group belonging and identity nor used phrases as imprecise as "the national imaginary."

But beginning with his landmark study *Philosophy and the Mirror of Nature* (1979), this sort of philosophy, which sought with ever greater precision and force to capture "reality" with a dispassionate mind and tools of rationality, lost its appeal for Rorty. What captured his attention—and soon his formidable philosophical talents—was good old American pragmatism, drawn primarily from John Dewey. Over the course of the 1980s, in a very writerly, though unfussy and even anhedonic kind of way (which earned him the nickname "Eeyore"), Rorty began reviving pragmatic theories to show the limits of analytic philosophy and the need for inquiry that can move beyond epistemology and back into the "problems of men [and women]." Rorty's point here was not necessarily to make philosophers more responsive to the needs of nonphilosophers, but to get Americans to readopt a way of thinking that could better help them meet the challenges of late twentieth-century life.

Ironically, Rorty became one of the most prominent and widely read living American philosophers by trying to even further circumscribe professional philosophers' influence on society. As he put it in 1986, "imagine . . . [that] you open your copy of the *New York Times* and read that the philosophers, in convention assembled, have unanimously agreed that values are objective, science rational, truth a matter of correspondence to reality" and that they "have adopted a short, crisp set of standards of rationality and morality." Rather than praise the heavens, Rorty surmised, readers would be outraged by their unilateralism and arrogance. For Rorty, this is as it should be. No matter how much Americans get involved in (and worry over) contestations of truth, beauty, morality, and justice, they do not really want philosophers—or any professional intellectuals for that matter—to settle the debates once and for all. That is what a totalitarian society looks like, not a vibrant, if messy, democratic one.

What Rorty proposed, in books including *Consequences of Pragmatism* (1982), *Contingency, Irony, and Solidarity* (1988), and *Achieving Our Country* (1998), was instead something he called "pragmatism," "left-wing Kuhnianism," "solidarity," and even "ethnocentrism," and he described practitioners of this way of antifoundational ethical and epistemological reasoning, like himself, as proud "fuzzies."[3] Rorty, following the American pragmatists and German antifoundationalists (most especially Nietzsche and Heidegger), insisted that there are no timeless absolutes of knowledge, no ethical universals, and that all discourses—humanistic, artistic, and even scientific (à la Kuhn)—are always invariably linguistically mediated and culturally dependent. Period. Full stop. If this was a difficult concept for James's and Dewey's contemporaries to understand or accept, it should no longer be the case with Rorty's contemporaries thanks in large part to Kuhn's *Structure of Scientific*

Revolutions (1962). After all, Kuhn had (to Rorty's mind at least) sufficiently demonstrated that even *science* isn't a privileged domain of objectivity, nor are its conclusions absolute truths corresponding to a timeless reality. Period. Full stop. As a result, argued Rorty, humanists and moralists should stop trying to ape a discredited notion of objective inquiry in their pursuits of peaceful, liberal communities.

But closing the accounts of foundationalism in no way meant foreclosing the promise of—and deep need for—a shared moral life in the United States, as well as a durable cosmopolitanism in an era of increased globalization. All Rorty suggested is that late twentieth-century aspiring problem solvers do it the way practicing scientists actually do it: by seeking "intersubjectivity" (mutual understanding between two or more subjective perspectives) rather than "objectivity," and "unforced agreement" as the basis for group solidarity rather than "truth." Rorty proudly referred to this way of solidarity-seeking problem solving as "ethnocentric," which, of course, raised the eyebrows of his critics on both the left and right. But what he meant was simply that there is nothing anyone can establish about truth that does not derive from some group's (whether one's own "ethnos" or another's "paradigm") customary ways of doing so. Rorty rejected calling this "relativism" and instead called it what it was, namely, "ethnocentrism"—not a "pig-headed refusal to talk to representatives of other communities," but rather a recognition that one's own community, as with all communities, works by its "own lights. . . . [E]thnocentrism is simply that there are no other lights to work by." Those lights will be idiosyncratic, perhaps even quirky, particular to that group's own history and experience. By the pragmatists' light, that is no problem at all; indeed, it is to be expected. All the pragmatist "fuzzies" hope for is that once people can recognize and even welcome the differences between the self and the group, and the group and other groups, they can try to cultivate cultures that foster private fulfillment and (inter)group "reciprocal loyalty" necessary for human flourishing.[4]

In his only autobiographical reflection, "Trotsky and the Wild Orchids" (1992), Rorty joked that if being considered a pariah by both the Left and the Right meant that a thinker was on to something, then he was probably "in good shape."[5] His list of friends and friendly and even unfriendly critics reads like a "who's who" of late twentieth-century thought: Jürgen Habermas, Martha Nussbaum, Jacques Derrida, Kwame Anthony Appiah, Alasdair MacIntyre, Cornel West, and Charles Taylor. Some took up similar foundation-free ethical positions on how to build liberal communities at home and around the world. Others shared his humane, liberal commitments but worried that he, like the early pragmatists before him, could not achieve them without a correspondence theory of truth. Some found the precision of his argumentation lacking and suggested that was why he was such a cultural hero among liberal humanists and lived in exile from his earlier tribe of analytic philosophers. Others disagreed, arguing that Rorty's epistemology was perfectly robust, but that it actually pointed him to antidemocratic positions, not the fuzzy liberalism he was after. But all could agree on the risks involved in his foundation-free, postmodern effort to "achieve," not inherit, an America that could be home to all Americans.

Postmodernist thought raised difficult, urgent questions then, and it remains to be seen what the answers are or if they will ever come. Should the United States be American citizens' primary allegiance, or in the era of globalization, should they aspire instead to be citizens of the world? If we cannot even get intergroup reciprocal loyalty in the United States, how can we possibly achieve it internationally? How can the nation safeguard its most precious ideals by way of solidarity and not truth? Has 9/11 proven this intellectual vision bankrupt once and for all, or has it only proven why it is our last best hope for a peaceful world? Until twenty-first-century Americans can find what William James called a "moral equivalent for war," they will—and should—keep posing these questions and collaborating to find answers. This intellectual collaboration is what British philosopher Michael Oakeshott hoped for when in 1959 he recommended "the conversation of mankind."[6]

Is the cause of America the cause of all mankind? And what is that cause after all? From distant glimmerings of "America" (the Waldseemüller map of 1507) to "City upon a Hill" and "Magnalia Christi Americana," into the nineteenth century with "American Scholar" and the "[slaves'] fourth of July," and continued throughout the twentieth century with "double-consciousness," "Trans-national America," "settlement ideal," "American Dream," "I have a dream," "Postethnic America," "Achieving . . . America," and the "heyday of the fuzzies," Americans have been trying to figure this out for quite some time. Over the course of the centuries, Americans learned and self-taught, native born and immigrant, religious and secular, and left and right have contributed to this long conversation by offering new arguments and key terms for Americans to think about the world, themselves, their truth, and their America. No one, so far, has been successful in answering these questions once and for all. They only came up with provisional explanations and then posed new questions. Perhaps we should not want it any other way. And so the conversation of American thought continues.

NOTES

Introduction

1. Ralph Ellison, *Invisible Man* (New York: Random House, 1952), 439.

Chapter 1

1. It is likely—though we cannot be sure—that the author was male.

2. Martin Waldseemüller, *The Cosmographiae Introductio of Martin Waldseemüller in Facsimile: Followed by The Four Voyages of Amerigo Vespucci, with Their Translation into English; to Which Are Added Waldseemüller's Two World Maps of 1507,* ed. Charles George Herbermann (New York: United States Catholic Historical Society, 1907), 70.

3. José de Acosta, as quoted in Anthony Grafton, April Shelford, and Nancy Siraisi, *New Worlds, Ancient Texts: The Power of Tradition and the Shock of Discovery* (Cambridge, MA: Belknap Press, 1995), 1.

4. Thomas Hobbes, *Leviathan; Or the Matter, Forme, & Power of a Commonwealth Ecclesiasticall and Civill,* ed. C. B. MacPherson (Baltimore: Penguin, 1985), 186–88.

5. Piambohou and Nehemiah, as quoted in John Eliot, *The Dying Speeches of Several Indians* (Cambridge, MA: Samuel Green, ca. 1685), 4, 8.

6. Father Jacques Marquette, as quoted in Louis Hennepin, *A New Discovery of a Vast Country in America* (1698; Chicago: A. C. McClurg & Co., 1903), 2:663.

7. Hugo Grotius, *On the Origin of the Native Races of America: A Dissertation* (Edinburgh: privately reprinted, [1642], Engl. trans. 1884), 17.

8. Anne Hutchinson, as quoted in David D. Hall, ed. *The Antinomian Controversy, 1636–1638: A Documentary History* (Middletown, CT: Wesleyan University Press, 1968), 319, 312, 337.

9. Jonathan Edwards, "Sinners in the Hands of an Angry God" (1741), in *Sinners in the Hands of an Angry God and Other Puritan Sermons* (Mineola, NY: Dover Thrift Edition, 2005), 178.

10. John Winthrop, "A Modell of Christian Charity" (1630), in *Early American Writing*, ed. Giles Gunn (New York: Penguin Books, 1994), 112.

11. Ibid., 108, 111.

12. Thomas Paine, *Common Sense* (1776; Minneola, NY: Dover Thrift Editions, 1997), 51.

Chapter 2

1. John Locke, *Two Treatises of Government*, ed. Peter Laslett, 3rd ed. (Cambridge: Cambridge University Press, 1988; originally published 1689), 301.

2. Denis Diderot, as quoted in Peter Gay, *The Enlightenment: An Interpretation; The Rise of Modern Paganism* (1966; New York: Norton, 1995), 142.

3. Thomas Jefferson to A Committee of the Danbury Baptist Association, January 1, 1802, in *The Life and Selected Writings of Thomas Jefferson*, ed. Adrienne Koch and William Peden (1944; New York: Modern Library, 2004), 307; and "howling atheist" as quoted in John Ferling, *Adams vs. Jefferson: The Tumultuous Election of 1800* (Oxford: Oxford University Press, 2004), 154.

4. George Washington, "Circular to the States" (1783), in *The Writings of George Washington from the Original Manuscript Sources, 1745–1799*, ed. John C. Fitzpatrick (Washington, DC: Government Printing Office, 1931–44), 26:485.

5. Ibid.

6. Thomas Reid, as quoted in Leigh Eric Schmidt, *Hearing Things: Religion, Illusion, and the American Enlightenment* (Cambridge, MA: Harvard University Press, 2000), 17; and John Locke, *An Essay Concerning Human Understanding*, ed. Peter H. Nidditch (Oxford: Oxford University Press, 1975), 146.

7. Jeremy Bentham, "Panopticon, or, The inspection-house containing the idea of a new principle of construction applicable to any sort of establishment, in which persons of any description are to be kept under inspection: and in particular to penitentiary-houses, prisons, houses of industry . . . and schools: with a plan of

management adapted to the principle: in a series of letters, written in the year 1787," in *The Works of Jeremy Bentham: Published under the Superintendence of His Executor, John Bowring* (Edinburgh: William Tait, 1843), 4:39.

8. Benjamin Franklin, as quoted in Jonathan Lyons, *The Society for Useful Knowledge: How Benjamin Franklin and Friends Brought the Enlightenment to America* (New York: Bloomsbury Press, 2013), 7, 50.

9. Immanuel Kant, "An Answer to the Question: 'What Is Enlightenment?'" in *Kant: Political Writings*, ed. H. S. Reiss (1970; Cambridge: Cambridge University Press, 2016), 54.

10. Milcah Martha Moore, *Miscellanies, Moral and Instructive, in Prose and Verse* (Philadelphia: Joseph James, 1787), 147.

11. Lord Kames, as quoted in Linda Kerber, "The Republican Mother: Women and the Enlightenment—An American Perspective," *American Quarterly* 28, no. 2 (Summer 1976): 196.

12. Locke, *Two Treatises of Government*, 319.

13. James Otis, as quoted in Linda Kerber, *Women of the Republic: Intellect and Ideology in Revolutionary America* (Chapel Hill: University of North Carolina Press, 1980), 30.

14. Judith Sargent Murray, "Letter to Reverend Redding," in *Judith Sargent Murray: A Brief Biography with Documents*, ed. Sheila L. Skemp (Boston: Bedford/St. Martin's, 1998), 175.

15. Thomas Jefferson, *Notes on the State of Virginia* (London: John Stockdale, 1787), 232, 272.

16. Benjamin Wadsworth, as quoted in Craig Steven Wilder, *Ebony and Ivy: Race, Slavery, and the Troubled History of America's Universities* (New York: Bloomsbury, 2013), 120.

17. Benjamin Franklin, *The Complete Works, in Philosophy, Politics, and Morals, of the Late Dr. Benjamin Franklin: Now First Collected and Arranged; With Memoirs of His Early Life, Written by Himself* (London: J. Johnson and Longman, Hurst, Reese, Orme, and Brown, 1806), 3:544.

18. Benjamin Franklin, *The Life of Benjamin Franklin, Containing the Autobiography* (Boston: Tappan and Dennet, 1844), 105.

19. John Adams to Hezekiah Niles, February 1818, in *The Works of John Adams, Second President of the United States: With a Life of the Author, Notes and Illustrations, by His Grandson Charles Francis Adams* (Boston: Little, Brown and Company, 1856), 10:282.

20. John Adams to Thomas Jefferson, February 3, 1812, in *The Adams-Jefferson Letters: The Complete Correspondence between Thomas Jefferson and Abigail and John Adams*, ed. Lester J. Cappon (1959; Chapel Hill: University of North Carolina Press, 1987), 295.

21. Hannah Arendt, *On Revolution* (New York: Viking Press, 1969), 196.

22. Thomas Paine, *Common Sense* (1776; New York: Dover, 2017), 31, 20.

23. Ibid., 11, 2.

Chapter 3

1. Ralph Waldo Emerson, "Historic Notes of Life and Letters in New England" (1883) in *The Transcendentalists: An Anthology*, ed. Perry Miller (1950; Cambridge, MA: Harvard University Press, 2001), 494.

2. J. Hector St. John de Crèvecœur, *Letters from an American Farmer* (1782; New York: Duffield and Co., 1908), 54.

3. Noah Webster, *Dissertations on the English Language* (Boston: Isaiah Thomas & Company, 1789), 179.

4. Noah Webster, *A Grammatical Institute of the English Language . . . Part I* (Hartford, CT: Hudson & Goodwin, 1783), 14.

5. Noah Webster, *An American Dictionary of the English Language* (New York: S. Converse, 1828), https://archive.org/details/americandictiona-01websrich.

6. Thomas Jefferson to John Adams, June 10, 1815, *The Adams-Jefferson Letters: The Complete Correspondence between Thomas Jefferson and Abigail and John Adams*, ed. Lester J. Cappon (1959; Chapel Hill: University of North Carolina Press, 1987), 443.

7. Thomas Paine, *Common Sense* (1776; New York: Dover, 2017), 10.

8. Thomas Paine to "a friend," May 12, 1797, in *The Writings of Thomas Paine*, ed. Moncure Daniel Conway (New York: G. P. Putnam's Sons, 1908), 4:198.

9. Thomas Paine, *Age of Reason* (1794–1795), in Conway, *Writings of Thomas Paine*, 4:34, 22, 190.

10. John Adams to Benjamin Rush, January 21, 1810, in *Old Family Letters: Copied from the Originals for Alexander Biddle* (Philadelphia: J. B. Lippincott Co., 1892), 251.

11. Theodore Parker, "A Discourse on the Transient and Permanent in Christianity" (1841; Boston: American Unitarian Association, 1908).

12. William Ellery Channing, "Unitarian Christianity" (1819), in *A Selection from the Works of William E. Channing, D.D.,* ed. W. Copeland Bowie (Boston: American Unitarian Association, 1855), 186, 211, 191.

13. William Ellery Channing, "The Moral Argument against Calvinism" (1820) in *A Selection from the Works of William E. Channing,* 287.

14. Ralph Waldo Emerson, "Divinity School Address" (1838), *Emerson: Essays and Lectures* (New York: Library of America, 1983), 80–81.

15. Ibid., 88–89.

16. Henry David Thoreau, *A Week on the Concord and Merrimack Rivers* (1849; New York: Penguin, 1998), 58.

17. Oliver Wendell Holmes Jr., as quoted in *The Legacy of Oliver Wendell Holmes, Jr.,* ed. Robert W. Gordon (Stanford, CA: Stanford University Press, 1992), 199.

18. Ralph Waldo Emerson, "The American Scholar" (1837), *Essays and Lectures,* 53, 66, 57, 53, 70.

19. Ibid., 53.

20. Ralph Waldo Emerson, "Self-Reliance" (1841), *Essays and Lectures,* 271.

21. Emerson, "American Scholar," 54.

22. Ralph Waldo Emerson, *Emerson in His Journals,* ed. Joel Porte (Cambridge, MA: Belknap Press 1982), 99.

23. George Fitzhugh, *Sociology for the South, Or the Failure of a Free Society* (Richmond, VA: A. Morris, 1854), 26.

24. Louisa S. McCord, "Negro-Mania," in *Political and Social Essays* (1852; Charlottesville: University of Virginia Press, 1995), 237.

25. Louisa S. McCord, "Enfranchisement of Woman," in *Political and Social Essays,* 110.

26. As quoted in Bruce M. Conforth, *African American Folksong and American Cultural Politics: The Lawrence Gellert Story* (Lanham, MD: Scarecrow Press, 2013), 191.

27. Emerson, "Self-Reliance," 260, 278; and Margaret Fuller, as quoted in Donna Dickenson, ed., *Margaret Fuller: Writing a Woman's Life* (New York: St. Martin's Press, 1993), 77.

Chapter 4

1. Henry James, *Hawthorne* (London: Macmillan, 1879), 144.

2. Frederick Douglass, "What, to the Slave, Is the Fourth of July?" (1852), in *Lift Every Voice: African American Oratory, 1787–1900,* ed. Philip Sheldon Foner and Robert J. Branham (Tuscaloosa: University of Alabama Press, 1998), 258.

3. Abraham Lincoln, "Address to the Young Men's Lyceum of Springfield" (1838), in *The Portable Abraham Lincoln,* ed. Andrew Delbanco (1992; New York: Penguin, 2009), 23.

4. Abraham Lincoln, "Address at Gettysburg, Pennsylvania" (1863) in Delbanco, *Portable Abraham Lincoln,* 323–24.

5. Charles Darwin, *On the Origin of Species* (1859; Mineola, NY: Dover, 2006), 307.

6. Louis Agassiz, review of *The Origin of Species, The American Journal of Science and Arts,* second series, 29 (1860): 144.

7. Louis Agassiz, *Essay on Classification* (1859; Cambridge: Belknap Press, 1962), 137.

8. Othniel C. Marsh, "Introduction and Succession of Vertebrate Life in America," *American Journal of Science and Arts,* 3rd ser., 14, no. 83 (1877): 337–38.

9. Darwin, *On the Origin of Species,* 307.

10. Charles Hodge, *What Is Darwinism?* (New York: Scribner, Armstrong, and Co., 1874), 177.

11. John Fiske, *Through Nature to God* (Boston: Houghton, Mifflin and Company, 1899), 65–66.

12. William James, *Pragmatism and the Meaning of Truth* (1907; Cambridge, MA: Harvard University Press, 1978), 35.

13. Robert G. Ingersoll, "The Gods" (1872), in *The Works of Robert G. Ingersoll,* (New York: C. P. Farrell, 1900), 7.

14. Ibid., 4:36.

15. William Graham Sumner, *War and Other Essays,* ed. Albert Galloway Keller (New Haven, CT: Yale University Press, 1911), 198.

16. Ibid., 177.

17. Thorstein Veblen, *The Theory of the Leisure Class: An Economic Study of Institutions* (New York: Macmillan Company, 1912), 188.

18. Ibid., 116, 98, 62, 6, 1, 200.

19. Matthew Arnold, *Culture and Anarchy, and Other Writings*, ed. Stefan Collini (1869; Cambridge: Cambridge University Press, 1993), 59, 79.

20. Horace Bushnell, *Women's Suffrage: The Reform against Nature* (New York: Charles Scribner and Co., 1869), 51.

21. Edwin Lawrence Godkin, *Reflections and Comments, 1865–1895* (New York: Charles Scribner's Sons, 1895), 201, 203.

22. George Santayana, *The Genteel Tradition in American Philosophy and Character and Opinion in the United States*, ed. James Seaton (New Haven, CT: Yale University Press, 2009), 5, 6, 9.

23. Henry David Thoreau, "A Plea for Captain John Brown" (1859), in *Walden and Other Writings*, ed. Brooks Atkinson (New York: Modern Library, 1992), 720–21.

Chapter 5

1. William James, *The Principles of Psychology*, vol. 1 (1890; New York: Dover, 1950), 488, and John Dewey, "The Influence of Darwinism on Philosophy" (1909), in *The Influence of Darwin on Philosophy: And Other Essays in Contemporary Thought* (New York: Henry Holt and Company, 1910), 1.

2. J. Estlin Carpenter, as quoted in Richard Hughes Seager, *The World's Parliament of Religions: The East/West Encounter, Chicago, 1893* (Bloomington: Indiana University Press, 1995), 69.

3. Frederick Jackson Turner, *The Frontier in American History* (1894; New York: Henry Holt and Company, 1920), 37.

4. Dewey, *Influence of Darwin on Philosophy*, 8–9, 13, 18.

5. Edward H. Madden, "Chance and Counterfacts in Wright and Peirce," *Review of Metaphysics* 9, no. 3 (March 1956): 420.

6. William James, "The Will to Believe," (1896) in *The Will to Believe and Other Essays in Popular Philosophy & Human Immortality: Two Supposed Objections to the Doctrine* (1897; New York: Dover, 1956), 11.

7. William James, "Remarks on Spencer's Definition of Mind as Correspondence," *Journal of Speculative Philosophy* 12, no. 1 (January 1878): 13.

8. William James, *Pragmatism and the Meaning of Truth* (1907; Cambridge, MA: Harvard University Press, 1978), 37.

9. William James, "On a Certain Blindness in Human Beings" (1899), in *Talks to Teachers on Psychology: And to Students on Some of Life's Ideals* (New York: Henry Holt and Company, 1914), 264.

10. John Dewey, *Problems of Men* (New York: Philosophical Library, 1946).

11. Walter Lippmann, *Drift and Mastery: An Attempt to Diagnosis of the Current Unrest* (1914; Madison: University of Wisconsin Press, 2015), 147.

12. Jane Addams, *Twenty Years at Hull House with Autobiographical Notes* (1910; New York: Macmillan, 1912), 124, 144; Jane Addams, "The Settlement as a Factor in the Labor Movement" (1895), in *The Jane Addams Reader*, ed. Jean Bethke Elshtain (New York: Basic Books, 2002), 56.

13. Edward A. Ross, "The Causes of Race Superiority," *Annals of the American Academy of Political and Social Science* 18 (July 1901): 88.

14. W. E. B. Du Bois, *The Souls of Black Folk* (1903; New Haven, CT: Yale University Press, 2015), 1, 5.

15. Franz Boas, "Museums of Ethnology and Their Classification," *Science* 9 (1887): 589.

16. Randolph Bourne, "Trans-National America" (1916), in *The Radical Will: Selected Writings, 1911–1918*, ed. Olaf Hansen (Berkeley: University of California Press, 1992), 259.

17. Randolph Bourne, "The Handicapped" (1911), in *Radical Will*, 78.

18. Randolph Bourne, "Trans-National America," in *Radical Will*, 260, 249, 250, 260, 263.

19. Randolph Bourne, "Twilight of Idols," in *Radical Will*, 337, 344.

Chapter 6

1. F. Scott Fitzgerald, *This Side of Paradise* (New York: Charles Scribner's Sons, 1920), 282.

2. Margaret Mead, *Coming of Age in Samoa: A Psychological Study of Primitive Youth for Western Civilization* (1928; New York: Harper Collins, 2001), 170.

3. Langston Hughes, "I, Too," in *The Collected Poems of Langston Hughes* (New York: Vintage Books, 1994), 46.

4. Walter Lippmann, *A Preface to Morals* (1929; New York: Routledge, 2017), 8.

5. Warren G. Harding, as quoted in Michael C. Parrish, *Anxious Decades: America in Prosperity and Depression, 1920–1941* (New York: W.W. Norton & Co., 1994), 9.

6. Margaret Sanger, *Woman and the New Race* (New York: Brentano's Publishers, 1920), 226, 35.

7. Margaret Sanger, *The Pivot of Civilization* (New York: Brentano's Publishers, 1922), 220, 179–81.

8. Lothrop Stoddard, "The Pedigree of Judah," *The Forum* 75, no. 3 (March 1926): 323.

9. Ezra Pound, "Hugh Selwyn Mauberley" (1920), in *Selected Poems of Ezra Pound* (New York: New Directions, 1957), 64.

10. Alain Locke, ed., *The New Negro* (1925; New York: Simon and Schuster, 1992), 9, 14.

11. W. E. B. Du Bois, *The Souls of Black Folk* (1903; New Haven, CT: Yale University Press, 2015), 3.

12. Ralph Waldo Emerson, "The Poet" (1844), in *Emerson: Essays and Lectures* (New York: Library of America, 1983), 450.

13. James Truslow Adams, *The Epic of America* (1931; New York: Routledge, 2012), 404.

14. Arthur M. Schlesinger Jr., *The Crisis of the Old Order, 1919–1933* (1957; Boston: Houghton Mifflin, 2003), 290.

15. Charles A. Beard, "The Myth of Rugged American Individualism," *Harper's Magazine* (December 1931), 22.

16. Rexford Tugwell, as quoted in Edward A. Purcell Jr., *The Crisis of Democratic Theory: Scientific Naturalism & the Problem of Value* (Lexington: University Press of Kentucky, 1973), 23, 35.

17. Walter S. Cook, as quoted in Laura Fermi, *Illustrious Immigrants: Intellectual Migration from Europe, 1930–41* (Chicago: University of Chicago Press, 1968), 78.

18. Thomas Mann, as quoted in Frederic Morton, "A Talk with Thomas Mann at 80," *New York Times*, June 5, 1955, BR6.

Chapter 7

1. "Editorial Statement," in *America and the Intellectuals: A Symposium*, ed. Newton Arvin (New York: Partisan Review, 1953), 5.

2. Lionel Trilling, in Arvin, *America and the Intellectuals*, 111.

3. Franklin D. Roosevelt, as quoted in John B. Hench, *Books as Weapons: Propaganda, Publishing, and the Battle for Global Markets in the Era of World War II* (Ithaca, NY: Cornell University Press, 2010), 5.

4. William Graebner, *The Age of Doubt: Thought and Culture in the 1940s* (Prospect Heights, IL: Waveland Press, 1998), xi.

5. C. P. Snow, *The Two Cultures* (Cambridge: Cambridge University Press, 2008), 3–4.

6. Reinhold Niebuhr, *The Irony of American History* (1952; Chicago: University of Chicago Press, 2008), 3.

7. Louis Hartz, *The Liberal Tradition in America: An Interpretation of American Political Thought since the Revolution* (New York: Harcourt Brace, 1955).

8. Peter Viereck, "Conservatism under the Elms," *New York Times*, November 4, 1951.

9. Peter Viereck, *Conservatism Revisited: The Revolt against Ideology* (1949; London and New York: Routledge, 2017), 105–30. (Note: Original subtitle of 1949 version was "Revolt against Revolt.")

10. Adrienne Koch, "Pragmatic Wisdom and the American Enlightenment," *William and Mary Quarterly* 18, no. 3 (July 1961): 325.

11. Max Horkheimer and Theodor Adorno, *Dialectic of Enlightenment: Philosophical Fragments*, ed. Gunzelin Schmid Noerr, trans. Edmund Jephcott (1944; Stanford, CA: Stanford University Press, 2002), xi, 18.

12. Russell Kirk, *The Conservative Mind: From Burke to Eliot* (1953; Washington, DC: Regnery Publishing, 2001), 476.

13. Lionel Trilling, *The Liberal Imagination: Essays on Literature and Society* (1950; New York: New York Review of Books, 2008), 260, xvi.

14. Viereck, *Conservatism Revisited*, 63; and Claes G. Ryn, "Peter Viereck and Conservatism" in Viereck, *Conservatism Revisited*, 31.

15. Viereck, *Conservatism Revisited*, 153.

16. Arthur M. Schlesinger Jr., *The Vital Center: The Politics of Freedom* (Boston: Houghton Mifflin Co., 1949).

17. David Riesman, *The Lonely Crowd: A Study of the Changing American Character*, 2nd ed. (1950; New Haven, CT: Yale University Press, 2001), 25.

18. C. Wright Mills, *White Collar: The American Middle Classes* (New York: Oxford University Press, 1951), 233–35, 111; and C. Wright Mills, *The Power Elite* (New York: Oxford University Press, 1956), 342.

19. Ralph Ellison, *Invisible Man* (New York: Random House, 1952), 3.

20. Richard Wright, *The Outsider* (1953; New York: HarperCollins, 1993), 157.

21. Paul Tillich, *The Courage to Be* (1952; New Haven, CT: Yale University Press, 2000), 186–90.

22. *Religion and the Intellectuals: A Symposium* (New York: Partisan Review, 1950), 5, 94, 17, 70–77.

23. Carl Jung, *Psychology and Religion* (New Haven, CT: Yale University Press, 1938), 3.

24. Carl Jung, *Memories, Dreams, Reflections* (1961; New York: Vintage, 1989), 335.

25. Fritjof Capra, *The Tao of Physics: An Exploration of the Parallels between Modern Physics and Eastern Mysticism* (Boulder, CO: Shambhala, 1975), 306.

26. John Barth, "The Literature of Exhaustion," in *The Friday Book: Essays and Other Nonfiction* (Baltimore: Johns Hopkins University Press, 1984), 62, 64, 67, 64, 75.

Chapter 8

1. Marshall McLuhan, *Understanding Media. The Extensions of Man* (1964; Cambridge: Massachusetts Institute of Technology Press, 1995), 7.

2. Marshall McLuhan, *The Gutenberg Galaxy: The Making of Typographic Man* (Toronto: University of Toronto Press, 1962), 5.

3. Jacques Derrida, *Of Grammatology*, trans. Gayatri Chakravorty Spivak (1967; Baltimore: Johns Hopkins University Press, 1997), 163.

4. Students for a Democratic Society, "Port Huron Statement" (1962), in Tom Hayden, *The Port Huron Statement: The Visionary Call of the 1960s Revolution* (New York: Thunder's Mouth Press, 2005), 53.

5. Milton Friedman, *Capitalism and Freedom* (Chicago: University of Chicago Press, 2002), 200.

6. Betty Friedan, *The Feminine Mystique* (1963; New York: W.W. Norton & Co., 2013), 1, 337.

7. Martin Luther King Jr., "Letter from Birmingham City Jail" (1963), in *A Testament of Hope: The Essential Writings and Speeches*, ed. James M. Washington (New York: HarperCollins, 2003), 292, 294–95, 292.

8. Jean-François Lyotard, *The Postmodern Condition: A Report on Knowledge*, trans. Geoff Bennington and Brian Massumi (1979; Minneapolis: University of Minnesota Press, 1984), xxiv.

9. Michel Foucault, *Discipline and Punish: The Birth of the Prison*, trans. Alan Sheridan (1977; New York: Random House, 1995), 82.

10. Allan Bloom, *The Closing of the American Mind* (1987; New York: Simon & Schuster, 2012), 154, 152, 151.

11. François Cusset, *French Theory: How Foucault, Derrida, Deleuze, & Co. Transformed the Intellectual Life of the United States*, trans. Jeff Fort (2003; Minneapolis: University of Minnesota Press, 2008), xvii.

12. Cornel West, *The American Evasion of Philosophy: A Genealogy of Pragmatism* (Madison: University of Wisconsin Press, 1989), 5.

13. Arthur M. Schlesinger Jr., *The Disuniting of America: Reflections on a Multicultural Society* (New York: W. W. Norton, 1991), 21.

14. Tom Wolfe, "The 'Me' Decade and the Third Great Awakening," *New York Magazine*, August 23, 1976, http://nymag.com/news/features/45938/.

15. Jimmy Carter, "The Crisis of Confidence," in *Jimmy Carter and the Energy Crisis of the 1970s. The Crisis of Confidence Speech of July 15, 1979: A Brief History with Documents*, ed. Daniel Horowitz (New York: Bedford St. Martins, 2004), x.

16. Vine Deloria Jr., *Custer Died for Your Sins: An Indian Manifesto* (New York: Macmillan, 1969), 1–2.

17. Audre Lorde, *Sister Outsider: Essays and Speeches* (Trumansburg, NY: Crossing Press, 1984), 114.

18. Judith Butler, *Gender Trouble* (1990; New York: Routledge, 1999), 6, 21, 33.

19. Kwame Anthony Appiah, *In My Father's House: Africa in the Philosophy of Culture* (New York: Oxford University Press, 1992), 81, 28, 38.

20. David Hollinger, *Postethnic America: Beyond Multiculturalism* (New York: Basic Books, 1995), 8.

21. Appiah, *In My Father's House*, 39.

22. Dinesh D'Souza, *The End of Racism: Principles for a Multiracial Society* (New York: Free Press Paperbacks, 1995), 528.

23. Chris Rock, as quoted in Anne M. Todd, *Chris Rock: Comedian and Actor* (New York: Chelsea House Publishers, 2006), 44.

24. bell hooks, "Postmodern Blackness," *Postmodern Culture* 1, no. 1 (September 1990): 9, 2, 11.

25. Thomas L. Haskell, "The Curious Persistence of Rights Talk in the 'Age of Interpretation,'" *Journal of American History* 74, no. 3 (December 1987): 984–1012.

26. Barbara Johnson, ed., *Freedom and Interpretation: The Oxford Amnesty Lectures 1992* (New York: Basic Books, 1993), 2.

Epilogue

1. Benedict Anderson, *Imagined Communities: Reflections on the Origin and Spread of Nationalism* (1983; New York: Verso, 2006), 7, 28, 24.

2. Holland Cotter, "Art of the AIDS Years: What Took Museums So Long?," *New York Times*, July 28, 2016, https://www.nytimes.com/2016/07/29/arts/design/art-of-the-aids-years-addressing-history-absorbing-fear.html.

3. Richard Rorty, "Science as Solidarity," in *The Rhetoric of the Human Sciences: Language and Argument in Scholarship and Public Affairs*, ed. John S. Nelson, Allan Megill, and Donald N. McClusky (Madison: University of Wisconsin Press, 1990), 50, 41–43.

4. Ibid., 42–43, 52.

5. Richard Rorty, "Trotsky and the Wild Orchids" (1992), in *Philosophy and Social Hope* (New York: Penguin, 1999), 3.

6. Michael Oakeshott, *The Voice of Poetry in the Conversation of Mankind* (London: Bowes & Bowes, 1959).

FURTHER READING

Abruzzo, Margaret N. *Political Pain: Slavery, Cruelty, and the Rise of Humanitarianism*. Baltimore: Johns Hopkins University Press, 2011.

Abzug, Robert H. *Cosmos Crumbling: American Reform and the Religious Imagination*. New York: Oxford University Press, 1994.

Armitage, David. *The Ideological Origins of the British Empire*. New York: Cambridge University Press, 2000.

Bailyn, Bernard. *The Ideological Origins of the American Revolution*. Cambridge, MA: Belknap Press, 1967.

Baker, Houston A. *Modernism and the Harlem Renaissance*. Chicago: University of Chicago Press, 1987.

Bay, Mia E. *The White Image in the Black Mind: African-American Ideas about White People, 1830–1925*. New York: Oxford University Press, 2000.

Bay, Mia E., Farah Jasmine Griffin, Martha S. Jones, and Barbara Dianne Savage. *Toward an Intellectual History of Black Women*. Chapel Hill: University of North Carolina Press, 2015.

Bederman, Gail. *Manliness and Civilization: A Cultural History of Gender and Race in the United States, 1880–1917*. Chicago: University of Chicago Press, 1996.

Biel, Steven. *Independent Intellectuals in the United States, 1910–1945*. New York: New York University Press, 1992.

Blake, Casey Nelson. *Beloved Community: The Cultural Criticism of Randolph Bourne, Van Wyck Brooks, Waldo Frank, and Lewis Mumford*. Chapel Hill: University of North Carolina Press, 1990.

Blight, David W. *Race and Reunion: The Civil War in American Memory*. Cambridge, MA: Belknap Press, 2002.

Bloch, Ruth H. *Visionary Republic: Millennial Themes in American Thought, 1756–1800*. New York: Cambridge University Press, 1985.

Borus, Daniel H. *Twentieth-Century Multiplicity: American Thought and Culture, 1900–1920*. Lanham, MD: Rowman & Littlefield, 2009.

Boyer, Paul S. *When Time Shall Be No More: Prophecy Belief in Modern American Culture*. Cambridge, MA: Belknap Press, 1992.

Bozeman, Theodore Dwight. *Protestants in an Age of Science: The Baconian Ideal and Antebellum American Religious Thought*. Chapel Hill: University of North Carolina Press, 1977.

Brick, Howard. *Age of Contradiction: American Thought and Culture in the 1960s*. New York: Twayne, 1998.

Brick, Howard. *Transcending Capitalism: Visions of a New Society in Modern American Thought*. Ithaca, NY: Cornell University Press, 2006.

Brown, Vincent. *The Reaper's Garden: Death and Power in the World of Atlantic Slavery*. Cambridge, MA: Harvard University Press, 2008.

Burgin, Angus. *The Great Persuasion: Reinventing Free Markets since the Depression*. Cambridge, MA: Harvard University Press, 2012.

Butler, Leslie. *Critical Americans: Victorian Intellectuals and Transatlantic Liberal Reform*. Chapel Hill: University of North Carolina Press, 2007.

Capper, Charles. *Margaret Fuller: An American Romantic Life*. Vol. 1, *The Private Years*. New York: Oxford University Press, 1992.

Capper, Charles. *Margaret Fuller: An American Romantic Life*. Vol. 2, *The Public Years*. New York: Oxford University Press, 2007.

Chaplin, Joyce. *Subject Matter: Technology, the Body, and Science on the Anglo-American Frontier, 1500–1676*. Cambridge, MA: Harvard University Press, 2003.

Chappell, David L. *A Stone of Hope: Prophetic Religion and the Death of Jim Crow*. Chapel Hill: University of North Carolina Press, 2004.

Cmiel, Kenneth. *Democratic Eloquence: The Fight over Popular Speech in Nineteenth-Century America*. New York: William Morrow, 1990.

Cohen-Cole, Jamie. *The Open Mind: Cold War Politics and the Sciences of Human Nature*. Chicago: University of Chicago Press, 2014.

Conn, Steven. *History's Shadow: Native Americans and Historical Consciousness in the Nineteenth Century*. Chicago: University of Chicago Press, 2004.

Cooney, Terry A. *Balancing Acts: American Thought and Culture in the 1930's*. New York: Twayne, 1995.

Cooper, Brittney C. *Beyond Respectability: The Intellectual Thought of Race Women*. Urbana: University of Illinois Press, 2017.

Coronado, Raúl. *A World Not to Come: A History of Latino Writing and Print Culture.* Cambridge, MA: Harvard University Press, 2013.

Cotkin, George. *Existential America.* Baltimore: Johns Hopkins University Press, 2003.

Cotlar, Seth. *Tom Paine's America: The Rise and Fall of Transatlantic Radicalism in the Early Republic.* Charlottesville: University Press of Virginia, 2011.

Croce, Paul Jerome. *Science and Religion in the Era of William James:* Vol. 1, *Eclipse of Certainty, 1820–1880.* Chapel Hill: University of North Carolina Press, 1995.

Curti, Merle. *The Growth of American Thought.* 3rd ed. New Brunswick, NJ: Transaction Publishers, 1982.

Cusset, François. *French Theory: How Foucault, Derrida, Deleuze, & Co. Transformed the Intellectual Life of the United States.* Translated by Jeff Fort. Minneapolis: University of Minnesota Press, 2008.

Dain, Bruce. *A Hideous Monster of the Mind: American Race Theory in the Early Republic* Cambridge, MA: Harvard University Press, 2003.

Degler, Carl N. *In Search of Human Nature: The Decline and Revival of Darwinism in American Social Thought.* New York: Oxford University Press, 1991.

Denning, Michael. *The Cultural Front: The Laboring of American Culture in the Twentieth Century.* London: Verso, 1998.

Dorrien, Gary. *The Making of American Liberal Theology: Idealism, Realism, and Modernity, 1900–1950.* Louisville, KY: Westminster John Knox Press, 2003.

Dorrien, Gary. *The Making of American Liberal Theology: Imagining Progressive Religion, 1805–1900.* Louisville, KY: Westminster John Knox Press, 2001.

Douglas, Ann. *Terrible Honesty: Mongrel Manhattan in the 1920s.* New York: Farrar, Straus and Giroux, 1995.

Faust, Drew Gilpin. *A Sacred Circle: Dilemma of the Intellectual in the Old South, 1840–1860.* Philadelphia: University of Pennsylvania Press, 1986.

Feldman, Stephen M. *American Legal Thought from Premodernism to Postmodernism: An Intellectual Voyage.* Oxford: Oxford University Press, 2000.

Fink, Leon. *Progressive Intellectuals and the Dilemmas of Democratic Commitment.* Cambridge, MA: Harvard University Press, 1997.

Flores, Ruben. *Backroads Pragmatists: Mexico's Melting Pot and Civil Rights in the United States.* Philadelphia: University of Pennsylvania Press, 2014.

Foner, Eric. *Free Soil, Free Labor, Free Men: The Ideology of the Republican Party before the Civil War.* 2nd ed. Oxford: Oxford University Press, 1995.

Fox, Richard Wightman. *Jesus in America: Personal Savior, Cultural Hero, National Obsession.* New York: HarperCollins, 2004.

Fox, Richard Wightman, and James T. Kloppenberg, eds. *A Companion to American Thought*. Oxford/Cambridge, MA: Blackwell, 1995.

Fox-Genovese, Elizabeth, and Eugene D. Genovese. *The Mind of the Master Class: History and Faith in the Southern Slaveholders' Worldview*. New York: Cambridge University Press, 2005.

Frederickson, George M. *The Black Image in the White Mind: The Debate on Afro-American Character and Destiny, 1817–1914*. 2nd ed. Middletown, CT: Wesleyan University Press, 1987.

Gaines, Kevin. *Uplifting the Race: Black Leadership, Politics, and Culture in the Twentieth Century*. 2nd ed. Chapel Hill: University of North Carolina Press, 1996.

Genter, Robert. *Late Modernism Art, Culture, and Politics in Cold War America*. Philadelphia: University of Pennsylvania Press, 2010.

Gilman, Nils. *Mandarins of the Future: Modernization Theory in Cold War America*. Baltimore: Johns Hopkins University Press, 2003.

Gilroy, Paul. *The Black Atlantic: Modernity and Double Consciousness*. Cambridge, MA: Harvard University Press, 1993.

Graebner, William. *The Age of Doubt: American Thought and Culture in the 1940s*. Boston: Twayne, 1991.

Grey, Edward G. *New World Babel: Languages and Nations in Early America*. Princeton, NJ: Princeton University Press, 1999.

Gura, Philip F. *American Transcendentalism: A History*. New York: Hill and Wang, 2008.

Hager, Christopher. *Word by Word: Emancipation and the Act of Writing*. Cambridge, MA: Harvard University Press, 1994.

Hall, David D. *Worlds of Wonder; Days of Judgment: Popular Religious Belief in Early New England*. Cambridge, MA: Harvard University Press, 1990.

Hartman, Andrew. *A War for the Soul of America: A History of the Culture Wars*. Chicago: University of Chicago Press, 2015.

Haselby, Sam. *The Origins of Religious Nationalism*. New York: Oxford University Press, 2015.

Haskell, Thomas L. *The Emergence of Professional Social Science: The American Social Science Association and the Nineteenth-Century Crisis of Authority*. Urbana: University of Illinois Press, 1977.

Hatch, Nathan O. *The Sacred Cause of Liberty: Republican Thought and the Millennium in Revolutionary New England*. New Haven, CT: Yale University Press, 1977.

Hedstrom, Matthew S. *The Rise of Liberal Religion: Book Culture and American Spirituality in the Twentieth Century*. New York: Oxford University Press, 2013.

Hoeveler, J. David. *The Postmodernist Turn: American Thought and Culture in the 1970s*. New York: Twayne, 1996.

Hofstadter, Richard. *Anti-Intellectualism in American Life*. New York: Vintage, 1963.

Hollinger, David A. *Postethnic America: Beyond Multiculturalism*. Rev. ed. New York: Basic Books, 2006.

Hollinger, David A., and Charles Capper, eds. *The American Intellectual Tradition*. 6th ed., 2 vols. New York: Oxford University Press, 2011.

Holloway, Jonathan Scott. *Jim Crow Wisdom: Memory and Identity in Black America since 1940*. Chapel Hill: University of North Carolina, 2013.

Horowitz, Daniel. *Betty Friedan and the Making of The Feminist Mystique: The American Left, the Cold War, and Modern Feminism*. Amherst: University of Massachusetts Press, 1998.

Howe, Daniel Walker. *The Political Culture of the American Whigs*. Chicago: University of Chicago Press, 1984.

Hughes, H. Stuart. *The Sea Change: The Migration of Social Thought, 1930–1965*. New York: Harper & Row, 1975.

Igo, Sarah E. *The Averaged American: Surveys, Citizens, and the Making of a Mass Public*. Cambridge, MA: Harvard University Press, 2007.

Isaac, Joel. *Working Knowledge: Making the Human Sciences from Parsons to Kuhn*. Cambridge, MA: Harvard University Press, 2012.

Isaac, Joel, James Kloppenberg, Michael O'Brien, and Jennifer Ratner-Rosenhagen, eds. *The Worlds of American Intellectual History*. New York: Oxford University Press, 2017.

Jacoby, Russell. *The Last Intellectuals: American Culture in the Age of Academe*. New York: Basic Books, 2000.

Jay, Martin. *A History of the Frankfurt School and the Institute of Social Research, 1923–1950*. Boston: Little, Brown, 1973.

Jewett, Andrew. *Science, Democracy, and the American University: From the Civil War to the Cold War*. Cambridge: Cambridge University Press, 2014.

Kaag, John. *American Philosophy: A Love Story*. New York: Farrar, Straus, Giroux, 2016.

Kazin, Alfred. *On Native Grounds: An Interpretation of Modern American Prose Literature*. 3rd ed. Orlando, FL: Harcourt Brace & Company, 1995.

Kazin, Michael. *American Dreamers: How the Left Changed a Nation*. New York: Vintage, 2011.

Kendi, Ibram X. *Stamped from the Beginning: The Definitive History of Racist Ideas in America*. New York: Nation Books, 2016.

Kerber, Linda K. *Women of the Republic: Intellect and Ideology in Revolutionary America*. Chapel Hill: University of North Carolina Press, 1997.

King, Richard H. *Race, Culture, and the Intellectuals: 1940–1970.* Washington, DC: Woodrow Wilson Center Press and Johns Hopkins University Press, 2004.

Kittelstrom, Amy. *The Religion of Democracy: Seven Liberals and the American Moral Tradition.* New York: Penguin, 2015.

Kloppenberg, James T. *Toward Democracy: The Struggle for Self-Rule in European and American Thought.* New York: Oxford University Press, 2016.

Knott, Sarah. *Sensibility and the American Revolution.* Chapel Hill: University of North Carolina Press, 2009.

Kuklick, Bruce. *The Rise of American Philosophy: Cambridge, Massachusetts, 1860–1930.* New Haven, CT: Yale University Press, 1979.

Kupperman, Karen Ordahl, ed. *America in European Consciousness, 1493–1750.* Chapel Hill: Omohundro Institute and University of North Carolina Press, 1995.

Landsman, Ned C. *From Colonials to Provincials: American Thought and Culture, 1680–1760.* New York: Twayne, 1997.

Lasch, Christopher. *The New Radicalism in America 1889–1963: The Intellectual as a Social Type.* New York: W. W. Norton & Company, 1997.

Lears, T. J. Jackson. *No Place of Grace: Antimodernism and the Transformation of American Culture, 1880–1920.* Chicago: University of Chicago Press, 1983.

Lepore, Jill. *The Name of War: King Philip's War and the Origins of American Identity.* New York: Vintage, 1999.

Levine, Lawrence. *Black Culture and Black Consciousness: Afro-American Folk Thought from Slavery to Freedom.* 30th anniversary ed. New York: Oxford University Press, 2007.

Levy, Jonathan. *Freaks of Fortune: The Emerging World of Capitalism and Risk in America.* Cambridge, MA: Harvard University Press, 2012.

Livingston, James. *The World Turned Inside Out: American Thought and Culture at the End of the 20th Century.* Lanham, MD: Rowman & Littlefield, 2010.

Maier, Pauline. *American Scripture: Making the Declaration of Independence.* New York: Vintage, 1998.

Matthews, Jean V. *Toward a New Society: American Thought and Culture, 1800–1830.* Boston: Twayne, 1991.

May, Henry Farnham. *The End of American Innocence: A Study of the First Years of Our Own Time, 1912–1917.* New York: Alfred A. Knopf, 1959.

McClay, Wilfred M. *The Masterless: Self and Society in Modern America.* Chapel Hill: University of North Carolina Press, 1994.

McDaniel, W. Caleb. *The Problem of Democracy in the Age of Slavery: Garrisonian Abolitionists and Transatlantic Reform*. Baton Rouge: Louisiana State University Press, 2013.

Menand, Louis. *The Metaphysical Club: A Story of Ideas in America*. New York: Farrar, Straus and Giroux, 2001.

Miller, Perry. *Errand into the Wilderness*. Cambridge, MA: Belknap Press, 1956.

Moses, Wilson Jeremiah. *The Golden Age of Black Nationalism, 1850–1925*. Hamden, CT: Archon Books, 1978.

Murphy, Paul V. *The Rebuke of History: The Southern Agrarians and American Conservative Thought*. Chapel Hill: University of North Carolina Press, 2001.

Nash, George H. *The Conservative Intellectual Movement in America since 1945*. 30th anniversary ed. Wilmington, DE: Intercollegiate Studies Institute, 2006.

Noll, Mark A. *America's God: From Jonathan Edwards to Abraham Lincoln*. New York: Oxford University Press, 2002.

Numbers, Ronald L. *Darwinism Comes to America*. Cambridge, MA: Harvard University Press, 1998.

O'Brien, Michael. *Conjectures of Order: Intellectual Life and the American South, 1810–1860*. Chapel Hill: University of North Carolina Press, 2004.

Parker, Kunal Madhukar. *Common Law, History, and Democracy in America, 1790–1900: Legal Thought before Modernism*. New York: Cambridge University Press, 2011.

Pells, Richard H. *Radical Visions and American Dreams: Culture and Social Thought in the Depression Years*. New York: Harper & Row, 1973.

Perry, Lewis. *Civil Disobedience: An American Tradition*. New Haven, CT: Yale University Press, 2013.

Perry, Lewis. *Intellectual Life in America: A History*. Chicago: University of Chicago Press, 1989.

Posnock, Ross. *Color and Culture: Black Writers and the Making of the Modern Intellectual*. Cambridge, MA: Harvard University Press, 2000.

Postel, Charles. *The Populist Vision*. New York: Oxford University Press, 2007.

Prince, K. Stephen. *Stories of the South: Race and the Reconstruction of Southern Identity, 1865–1915*. Chapel Hill: University of North Carolina Press, 2014.

Purcell, Edward A., Jr. *The Crisis of Democratic Theory: Scientific Naturalism and the Problem of Value*. Lexington: University Press of Kentucky, 1973.

Rakove, Jack N. *Original Meanings: Politics and Ideas in the Making of the Constitution*. New York: Alfred A. Knopf, 1996.

Ratner-Rosenhagen, Jennifer. *American Nietzsche: A History of an Icon and His Ideas*. Chicago: University of Chicago Press, 2012.

Reuben, Julie A. *The Making of the Modern University: Intellectual Transformation and the Marginalization of Morality*. Chicago: University of Chicago Press, 1996.

Reynolds, David S. *Beneath the American Renaissance: The Subversive Imagination in the Age of Emerson and Melville*. New York: Random House, 1988.

Richter, Daniel K. *Facing East from Indian Country: Native History of Early America*. Cambridge, MA: Harvard University Press, 2001.

Rivett, Sarah. *The Science of the Soul in Colonial New England*. Chapel Hill: Omohundro Institute and University of North Carolina Press, 2011.

Roberts, Jon H. *Darwinism and the Divine in America: Protestant Intellectuals and Organic Evolution, 1859–1900*. Madison: University of Wisconsin Press, 1988.

Robin, Corey. *The Reactionary Mind: Conservatism from Edmund Burke to Sarah Palin*. New York: Oxford University Press, 2011.

Rodgers, Daniel T. *Age of Fracture*. Cambridge, MA: Belknap Press, 2011.

Rodgers, Daniel T. *Contested Truths: Keywords in American Politics since Independence*. New York: Basic Books, 1987.

Rose, Anne C. *Transcendentalism as a Social Movement, 1830–1850*. New Haven, CT: Yale University Press, 1986.

Rosenberg, Rosalind. *Beyond Separate Spheres: The Intellectual Roots of Modern Feminism*. New Haven, CT: Yale University Press, 1982.

Rosenfeld, Sophia A. *Common Sense: A Political History*. Cambridge, MA: Harvard University Press, 2011.

Ross, Dorothy. *The Origins of American Social Science*. Cambridge: Cambridge University Press, 1991.

Rubin, Joan Shelley, and Scott E. Casper, eds. *The Oxford Encyclopedia of American Cultural and Intellectual History*. 2 vols. Oxford: Oxford University Press, 2013.

Schmidt, Leigh Eric. *Hearing Things: Religion, Illusion, and the American Enlightenment*. 2nd ed. Cambridge, MA: Harvard University Press, 2002.

Schultz, Kevin M. *Tri-Faith America: How Catholics and Jews Held Postwar America to Its Protestant Promise*. New York: Oxford University Press, 2011.

Sehat, David. *The Myth of American Religious Freedom*. New York: Oxford University Press, 2011.

Shain, Barry. *The Myth of American Individualism: The Protestant Origins of American Political Thought*. Princeton, NJ: Princeton University Press, 1994.

Shalhope, Robert E. *The Roots of Democracy: American Thought and Culture, 1760–1800*. Boston: Twayne, 1990.

Shi, David E. *Facing Facts: Realism in American Thought and Culture, 1850–1920*. New York: Oxford University Press, 1995.

Shields, David S. *Civil Tongues and Polite Letters in British America*. Chapel Hill: Omohundro Institute and University of North Carolina Press, 1997.

Sicherman, Barbara. *Well-Read Lives: How Books Inspired a Generation of American Women*. Chapel Hill: University of North Carolina Press, 2010.

Singal, Daniel Joseph. *The War Within: From Victorian to Modernist Thought in the South, 1919–1945*. Chapel Hill: University of North Carolina Press, 1982.

Sklansky, Jeffrey. *Sovereign of the Market: The Money Question in Early America*. Chicago: University of Chicago Press, 2017.

Smith-Rosenberg, Carroll. *Disorderly Conduct: Visions of Gender in Victorian America*. New York: Oxford University Press, 1986.

Staloff, Darren. *The Making of an American Thinking Class: Intellectuals and Intelligentsia in Puritan Massachusetts*. New York: Oxford University Press, 1998.

Stanley, Amy Dru. *From Bondage to Contract: Wage Labor, Marriage, and the Market in the Age of Slave Emancipation*. Cambridge: Cambridge University Press, 1998.

Stansell, Christine. *American Moderns: Bohemian New York and the Creation of a New Century*. New York: Henry Holt, 2000.

Stauffer, John L. *The Black Hearts of Men: Radical Abolitionists and the Transformation of Race*. Cambridge, MA: Harvard University Press, 2004.

Stevenson, Louise L. *The Victorian Homefront: American Thought and Culture, 1860–1880*. New York: Twayne, 1991.

Tompkins, Jane. *Sensational Designs: The Cultural Work of American Fiction, 1790–1860*. New York: Oxford University Press, 1985.

Turner, James C. *Without God, without Creed: The Origins of Unbelief in America*. Baltimore: Johns Hopkins University Press, 1986.

Volk, Kyle G. *Moral Minorities and the Making of American Democracy*. New York: Oxford University Press, 2014.

Wall, Wendy L. *Inventing the "American Way": The Politics of Consensus from the New Deal to the Civil Rights Movement*. New York: Oxford University Press, 2008.

Walls, Laura Dassow. *The Passage to Cosmos: Alexander von Humboldt and the Shaping of America*. Chicago: University of Chicago Press, 2009.

Werth, Barry. *Banquet at Delmonico's: Great Minds, the Gilded Age, and the Triumph of Evolution in America.* New York: Random House, 2009.

Westbrook, Robert B. *John Dewey and American Democracy.* Ithaca, NY: Cornell University Press, 1993.

Wilder, Craig Steven. *Ebony and Ivy: Race, Slavery, and the Troubled History of America's Universities.* New York: Bloomsbury Press, 2013.

Wills, Garry. *Lincoln at Gettysburg: The Words That Remade America.* New York: Touchstone, 1992.

Winterer, Caroline. *American Enlightenments: Pursuing Happiness in the Age of Reason.* New Haven, CT: Yale University Press, 2016.

Wood, Gordon S. *The Creation of the American Republic, 1776–1787.* Chapel Hill: University of North Carolina Press, 1969.

Worthen, Molly. *Apostles of Reason: The Crisis of Authority in American Evangelicalism.* New York: Oxford University Press, 2014.

INDEX

Otis, James, 39
Outsider, The (1953). *See* Wright,
    Richard

Paine, Thomas, 29, 48, 57–59
Parker, Theodore, 61
Partisan Review, 134, 146
Peabody, Elizabeth Parker, 61, 66
Pearl Harbor, 132
Peirce, Charles Sanders, 104–5
Perennial Philosophy, The (1945).
    See Huxley, Aldous
Perkins, Frances, 128
phantasmagoria, 36
philosophy, 1, 3, 15, 26–27, 32,
    63–64, 94, 101, 103–7, 135,
    137, 142–49, 163, 169, 176–77;
    and deconstruction, 155, 159–
    60, 171; and empiricism, 30,
    104–6, 112; and existentialism,
    143–45; and pragmatism, 97,
    103–10, 114–15, 123, 137, 147,
    163–64, 176–79. *See also*
    Europe/European: thought
    (general); postmodernism
Philosophy and the Mirror of Nature
    (1979). *See* Rorty, Richard
physics, 112
Pirsig, Robert, 155
Pivot of Civilization, The (1922).
    See Sanger, Margaret
Plato, 27, 135
pluralism/multiculturalism.
    See culture/cultural
    criticism: pluralism
Poe, Edgar Allan, 143
"Poet, The" (1844). *See* Emerson,
    Ralph Waldo
poetry, 2, 32, 39, 62, 65, 101,
    117, 122–25, 142, 166. *See*
    also Hughes, Langston;
    Whitman, Walt

Poetry (magazine), 122
political theory, 2, 30, 32, 46–50, 84,
    131, 137–41, 156, 175–79
polygenesis. *See* evolution/
    evolutionary theory
"Port Huron Statement, The" (1962).
    See Students for a Democratic
    Society, The (SDS)
postcolonialism, 4
Postmodern Condition, The (1979). *See*
    Lyotard, Jean-François
postmodernism, 151, 159–71, 179
Pound, Ezra, 122
power: human agency, 52, 115,
    137, 160–62, 167; language,
    5, 160, 167. *See also* empires/
    imperialism
Power Elite, The (1956). *See* Mills,
    C. Wright
Prabhavananda, Swami, 147
Prae-Adamitae (1655). *See* La
    Peyrère, Isaac
pragmatism. *See* philosophy:
    pragmatism
*Pragmatism: A New Name for Some
    Old Ways of Thinking* (1907). *See*
    James, William
Price, Dick, 149
Princeton University, 37, 81, 163
Principia (1687). *See*
    Newton, Isaac
Principles of Psychology, The (1890). *See*
    James, William
print culture, 18–19, 46, 48, 53–59, 94,
    110, 134–36, 139, 154–55, 175.
    See also republic of letters
Profit Over People (1999). *See*
    Chomsky, Noam
progressivism/Progressive movement,
    100, 103, 108–15, 124, 128, 136,
    138, 156, 164
Prophet, The (1923). *See* Gibran, Kahlil